MASTERING MYSELF

A SECRET TO SUBDUE HELL BENT POWERS

Hemanth Kumar Makkena

First Published in March 2022

ISBN: 978-93-93388-97-1

BLUEROSE PUBLISHERS

www.bluerosepublishers.com

info@bluerosepublishers.com

+91 8882 898 898

Cover Design:

Geetika

Typographic Design:

Namrata Saini

Distributed by: BlueRose, Amazon, Flipkart

Dedication

Who will take the blame? Not I, will be the answer. You ask again and again; you will hear the same response. Ages will pass and the questioning being will disappear from the face of the earth, but still, it will continue to remain an unanswered question. Who wants to be credited for this? Who wants to be thanked? Who should be the gratitude expressed? Its I, its I, its I will be the echoing answer from all corners of the world.

It is not strange, neither is something new, but an age-old practice that man always plays blame game, whether needed or needless. For some, it is strength; for some, it is a weapon, but for almost all it is a savior. Washing linen, mainly dirty but in others' laundries is the general practice and common nature of human beings.

Therefore, wishing not to blame anyone and wishing not to make anybody accountable, I wish to plainly move ahead expressing my heartfelt gratitude to hundreds and thousands of people that I came across in my life so far with the same number of expressions, emotions, actions, reactions, provocations, strife, quarrels, fights, animosity, grudges, hate, etc. Since this book primarily and fundamentally deals with being blamed but not blaming, I hold myself responsible for all the fiery, wild, untamed, arrogant, harsh, mannerless, rude, angry, mad, frustrating, irritating, annoying, etc. nature, character and behavior.

Having faced numerous hard attacks, life threatening action-reaction way of living, but not before having losses in all areas of life except for winning fights, quarrels, arguments, I felt the need to put an end to all those mighty, mad, violent and destructive powers. This part of realization came with a price, better late than never, but doing this and succeeding to destroy the destructive forces, energies, strengths and powers is neither easy nor a known art, skill, ability, talent or a piece of learning. Again, neither can it be an achievement through some regular learning nor through meditation and some arts of living, but only with realization and with the help of some force, inspiration, motivation whether natural or supernatural.

Wishing to become a cool, calm, good natured gentleman, and the timely encounter with my Lord and my Savior Jesus Christ, who demands a life imitating Him, the only worthy qualification to be received by Him in His heavenly kingdom, I started giving up all that is against His Word and adopting all that is needed to follow Him and be with Him. In addition to this, being a husband, a father, a child of my parents, a sibling, a Priest of my congregation, a teacher of my students, friend of thousands etc. demanded my attitude, nature, character to be changed, in fact transformed into a pleasing personality.

Thus, I dedicate this piece of billions worth literature, that came with huge price and decades long experience to all the above listed unnamed individuals, who holds high place in my heart and are the reason to take me through all the colors and shades of life. I owe my entire life, my all, my everything to my Lord, my Savior Jesus Christ, who not just demands a clean life but also enables man to take up that path, and Himself guides, leads, helps and looks after the transformational process personally.

Therefore, the Master of Mastering Myself other than me is none other than my Master, My God. I wish and pray that not just this book, your tireless efforts, dedication, commitment to achieve the best in your life but also Christ personally shape you according to your need and His desire!

Foreword

Hemanth Makkena is seen by many as a successful Motivator and Entrepreneur, a symbol of progress and a messenger of inspiration to millions of people. What really qualifies him, however is a Self-discovery and Mastering Self. Mastering Myself is the one that gave him success on helping humans to be in charge of themselves. Most of the lessons he acquired in life were through his own experiences.

AS A PROFESSIONAL

Hemanth Makkena DHMCT, MDiv. Ex Principal of Hotel Management College is a think tank, keen observer, researcher, learner, educator, passionate explorer of happiness in the midst of happy, peaceful and joyous life. He pursues happiness in the midst of Happenings. He loves to add colors bright and beautiful, also strives to be the light house for every life that longs, struggle to reach the happy shores and find meaning for life.

AS A RESEACHER

He spends most of his time in the study of human mind, behavior, psychology, and entire development. Adding more fragrance to his special areas of learnings and researches, he came with different attention, view point and methodologies to have smiling and laughing families along with unique parental approaches, the kind of very first and the only.

AS AN AUTHOR

HEMANTH MAKKENA, Is an acclaimed and sought-after author. Mastering Myself is his third book. The author has also penned two other books on life and its challenges. Following them will lead to the world of happiness and controller of all human inner and outer powers. These books providing full understanding of self and others have already hit the stores.

A LENS THAT ZOOMS THE HAPPY WORLD

SIMPLY KIDDING, 33 Steps for Ideal Parenting.

I don't limit my words to suggest you for a buy of all the three and many more upcoming books, which are one of the musts buys that can bring you total happiness of life.

WHAT TO EXPECT

Now following all the experience that he has with his commitment and dedication to mankind, Mastering Myself is a must have. In this book you will discover that Hemanth has one mouth but he needs ten mouths because he is like a Niagara Falls and 12-inch stream. Exploding with wisdom that can move one from one dimension of life to the other, he deals deeply with stuff that people over look yet keeps them in bondage.

In this book, the author teaches you how not to play a blame game but take up responsibility of your actions in order to master yourself. One thing that makes one to be more expectant is the title of the book itself. Who on earth will not like to Master him or herself, based on the previous writings that were warmly welcomed by the world, this one too cannot be different? What I love about Hemanth is that this book covers all, all genders, all races and colors, young and old. As long as you have life you need this book, Mastering Myself – A Secret To Subdue Hell Bent Powers

EZEKIEL TSHABALALA,

Speaker, Teacher and Motivator, South Africa.

Preface

The need for another piece of writing, an advice, some more literature can never fade away from the lives of the humans on millions and billions of themes, topics, subjects and the repeat of the same. It could be need based, it could be through an inspiration, it could be an innovative and creative work, it could be a discovery, it could be an exploration, it could be an experience, it could be something, anything or everything else, but the literature never halted to enter the writer's and reader's world.

Mastering Myself is one in that ocean of billions of books and tons of literature. This is purely a need based, discovery, innovative, creative, explorative work of the author that stands in the gap between man and his unfulfilled needs and requirements, unachieved grip over internal powers, forces, energies, strengths and control systems. The author, who personally had been through bricks and bats; fires and waters; heavens and hells; lefts and rights; good and bad times, happenings, encounters, deliberate, accidental situations of life wished to bring this handy tool, a reflective literature in very easy and understandable language and approach to the reader, mainly the sufferer.

Many are the areas of life, especially inner ones, very strong, mighty and mad forces that usually appear man friendly but in reality, are foes and destroyers. Not everyone can realize this and not everyone can have the idea and understanding of it, but each and every one passes through these flames all through their lives. Apart from the personal experience, the author being in the field of care and counseling for nearly two decades thought penning down the exercise material would be the ideal way to address and cater to the needs of multitudes at a time in a very effective manner.

This book comes in two parts. The first one deals with the discovery part and the second with needed actions. Since this is an experiment, observation and result oriented work, and also the teaching, training and following practical material, the author emboldens his voice with loud vocals, suggesting that every individual consider it as a must have trainer at every home, institution, office, firm etc.

Handling emotions and holding wrong expressions from popping out forcibly, wild powers maddening the brains, mind and engulfing the bodies, roping in the nostrils of sickening mentalities and mean minds, cutting the nerves of racing unlawful desires and wishes, in a nutshell mastering one's own inner world consisting millions and billions of thought and action areas that are man's enemy but appear friendly at first sight can be made easy and the reader a bold claimant of Mastering Myself.

Acknowledgement

The first and the foremost ones to be acknowledged and thanked is my readers and my followers on WhatsApp, Facebook and other personal platforms. This work initially came in the single page reading for 44 days regularly, which later took the chapters form in the book, altogether consisting 44 chapters.

I owe my heartfelt thanks and gratitude to all the fore-mentioned individuals. Your responses, feedbacks, encouragements and constant demand to write more and more had put a blazing fire in my bosom, which kindled in giving the world a book called Mastering Myself- A Secret To Subdue Hell Bent Powers.

I am also very thankful to all the people who followed my advices, were been a part of my physical platforms, my congregation, individual counseling and one to one interaction. My sincere thanks also get an extended hand to Bishop Tshabalala from South Africa, my dear friend, a teacher, speaker and a motivator, who went through the entire manuscript and also agreed to endorse my writings through the foreword of this book.

I appreciate the availability of my wife Rebekah Hemanth Kumar Makkena and her willingness and attention to be an overseer of all my writings by going through the full script for proof reading and also suggesting valuable additions, deletions and changes. My son Joash Marvel Makkena also to be mentioned here for being instrumental in his capacity of suggestions and help.

Lastly, but not the least, rather the most important ones to be acknowledged here is each and every reader and practitioner of this unique book, Mastering Myself. I am very much indebted to Bluerose Publishers for agreeing to publish my book.

Above all, I thank my Lord and my Savior Jesus Christ, who is not only the source, inspiration, guide but also the transformer of my life.

Table of Contents

Lesson 1
Discovering Myself

'Life Inside The Ring – Whip In Your Hand'

Life is nothing but a game of names and numbers, their qualities and quantities, their conditions and situations. Remake and develop are exceptional in terms of material, finances and assets. Whereas repair, adjust and get used to the present levels of health are its conditional steps upon personal breakdown.

It is uncertain and unpredictable to the most, because it is basically dependent on moods and moves. And the moods and moves are subjective and relative to wealth and health. Everything is relative and purely fundamental on highs and lows of the spirit. In a nutshell, man is nothing but a producer of madness and happiness, and life is nothing but it's relative poverty and prosperity.

Enrolled in an automobile workshop for internship, the intern faces grave difficulties initially and the instructor finds it challenging, because the intern has no basic idea of the tools, its functions, automobiles, their conditions and the issues for which they were brought to garage for repair. In other words, he doesn't know the names of the tools and of the works.

Upon understanding the root cause, the instructor decided to be patient, slow, and knew that teaching names, functions and conditions of tools and automobiles is the right and effective way of training. After little dedicated time, the intern understood all that available there and learnt all the happenings too.

Since, it is all about names and numbers, let's be slow, patient, and learn who actually man is, what is he composed of, all the functions, conditions, moods and moves. But before moving there, the fundamental question is, do you have a basic idea, what is mastering myself? Do you feel that you are not master of yourself, but a workman, a slave, speechless, helpless and hopeless puppet under various powers, pressures, and uncontrollable negative, yourself?

If so, then the following chapters will take you to the coolest and calm levels of facing and dealing life with ease, empower you to attain the most powerful power called peace, which is way far away from everyone, and almost the entire human race hankers, cries, pleads and yells asking where can I find it? Can someone please let me know how can I find it?

You have heard or you may be the one, who often beg, demand, or fight to leave you alone in peace. You have everything but no peace of mind, it sounds meaningless and worthless gain of all the possessions. A troublesome life is impossible to enjoy unless learnt how to cope up with every situation and know how to enjoy even in times of loss, sufferings and calamities.

Art of mastering oneself and having the grip to gain, retain peace and share the same with others doesn't come easily and also cannot be purchased or possessed with monetary exchanges. We must bear in mind that, no skill, talent, art, ability and capability can be obtained in exchange of material or financial values, rather, they must be learned, developed, and mastered. As we proceed further, it is a heartfelt wish that, you become the ring master with the whip in your hand and life play the submissive role for your commands inside the ring!

Lesson 2
Discovering Myself

'Introducing Diffusers – Proving Newton Wrong'

The worlds are classified into visible-invisible, existing-nonexistent, faith based, mythological etc. The one who doesn't believe other than visible and existent invisible, lives a life of no faith on God, angels, religion, rebirth, resurrection, or moksha (deliverance).

Leaving the faith portion to religious institutes, saints, spiritual leaders etc., let us strictly limit our world to the visible physical and invisible existent powers, most importantly to the thought worlds, their actions and reactions.

Everything begins with thought, translating later into speech, script and action. If all the thoughts are good, then every speech, script and action will obviously be good too. If the thought itself is bad/wrong then the rest of the translation will be worse and worst. No good or bad thought and its translations is limited to you alone but is related to a part of or the entire world associated with you.

Hence, the natural law of nature needs to be modified and restated with correction here, that it is not for universal application, neither it is equal in force nor is similar in opposite nature. Since, we are dealing with man, mind, moods, moves, management, our focus is on diffusers.

Therefore, we restate that, 'not every action has equal and opposite reaction, but every action has equal/greater/lesser and similar/opposite/different reaction. If you have installed diffusers in your heart, then your mind will react suppressing/destroying the first force that hits you, but if you have installed reactors/explosives in your heart, then the force reacting against the first force obviously will be greater, quarrelsome, fighting, destructive and violent.

Mastering myself is for those who want to install or installed diffusers. It doesn't mean this is useless for the reactors. This is very well a transformational move for them to throw away the reactors/explosives and pickup diffusers. Need to bear a fact in mind here, that neither the diffusers are weak nor the reactors are strong. They are both great powers and strengths but opposite to each other.

Diffusers after some struggles find peace and sail on still waters for the rest of life, whereas reactors will have no end to conflicts, are insecure throughout and often willfully throw themselves into dirty waters, but the struggle to swim and reach offshore never happens. In fact, every stroke makes the waters murkier and stinky, and their lives have no scope to breathe in peace. Wish that you have good quality diffusers as we move ahead.

Lesson 3
Discovering Myself

'Cemented Walls – Still Waters Mirror'

Ancient, neither outdated nor unimportant but perfectly up to the mark and most importantly meaningful, beautiful and so lovely were those days of yesteryears, where almost everything was limited, unadulterated, pure, healthy and real. Today we have entered into unlimited and easily accessible modes, where except the 'lie' everything else is a 'lie'. You read it right, only the lie is true and everything else is false. Take any field, even the truth teaching saints keep their flocks away from it and present the lie that suits them as the ultimate truth.

Go to the markets, not every market has the same quality, they differ from high to low class income groups. The foods, the goods the markets/bazars provide for low and middle class are mere quantities but not qualities. Not only that, there is too much of fooling, cheating and looting. Meet any person, the amount of talk in the conversation/deal is either false, fake, lie, deception or selfish. Fueled by such mean mentality, most of the mankind doesn't want to be corrected, exposed or listen to the truth about them, which actually is contrast to their build up.

Mirrors of the old were not the sparkling and richly decorated pieces of glass, but were the still waters, shiny steel/metal surfaces. But most trustworthy than the former were the eyes of the people around them. People were groomed and adorned by the family members in the poor and middle class, by the servants/maids in the rich and royal class.

Though, any individual after or while grooming oneself asks the approval of others, whether it is perfectly done and looking good or not. Which means, the world of olden days completely trusted the declaration of others, where its natural eye cannot reach.

The question today that must trigger here is, 'how do you receive the declarations of the people about you? How kind/unkind are you after listening contrary to your claims/beliefs?'

Moving further, who do you think you are? What are you installed with? Are you angry, harsh, stiff, violent, stubborn, abusive, short tempered etc. or opposite to these? Do you have someone, who can show you the mirror, the truth? If not, you have just erected cemented walls that hides everything from the world and never allows world to see you.

Does that mean to have transparent see-through glass homes? Certainly not, but have at least one small mirror, a mirroring friend or critic and accept what it/he says. Hoping to see you mirrored, the basic essential element before we move to the next step of discovering myself!

Lesson 4
Discovering Myself

'Baby Reactors - Saintly Diffusers'

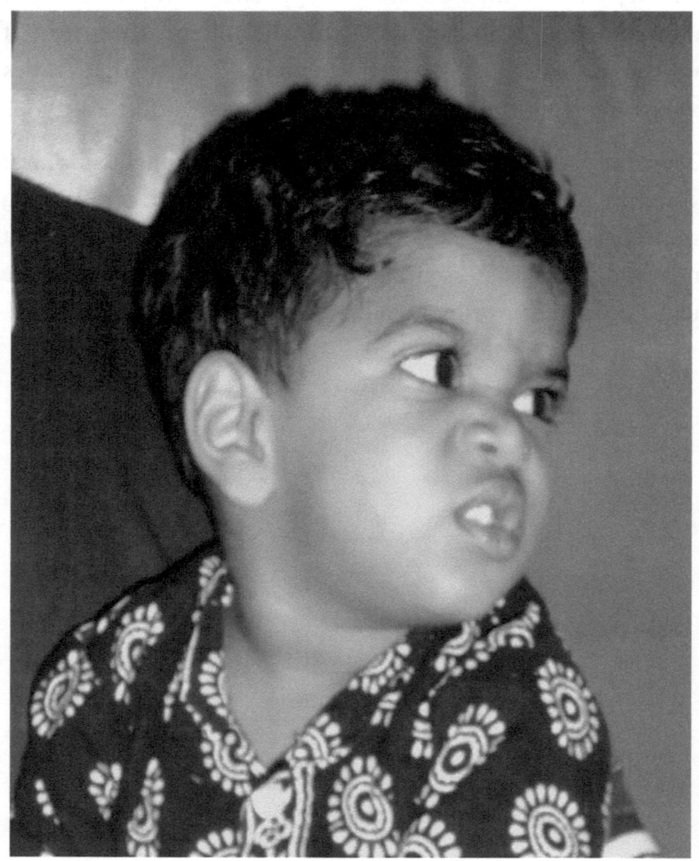

Call them 'baby reactors - saintly diffusers,' nothing is strange or new. Dealing with the diffusers and reactors, there's undeniable/unavoidable need to reach the roots as to know when, who and how they were installed. A field neglected, a path unused can easily catch up the wild greens, that intends to restrict their ultimate purposes, and occupy the complete area renaming, redefining, and authorizing themselves as wild and dangerous.

No doubt, greens look beautiful and attractive, but such types actually are harmful and dangerous too. It is not easy to walk on the wild which once was a field and a path, because there is always fear that some harmful creatures/animals might be dwelling there, which could be predators too.

Any surface, any dwelling place, or any vehicle is regular but careful at usage, will have perfect, clean and healthy life. Unused or unattended anything will soon and easily get spoiled. Therefore, any baby or adult, if not visited regularly with value systems, might turn fatal like the wild greens. No one knows what is inside the bush unless it comes out to get hold of its prey.

Similarly, unless a person exposes him/herself no one will know how wild, dangerous had their inner self turned. As the opening lines state baby reactors and saintly diffusers, it is widely believed that diffusers are basically for the old, the saintly and also to particular religiously faith-based group of people. The fact is, every baby is naturally born with the reactors or adapted soon after the birth.

The corrective action methodologies at home are reactive to the reactors. Hot blooded, angry, aggressive and short-tempered house cannot provide diffusers at home, just like no ordinary/common man's house has the provision for fire extinguishers. Therefore, it is obvious that baby reactors have the fuel abundantly available to increase the heat.

Have you wondered at the days old baby's angry reaction? Nothing strange. Isn't it? If anyone has cool mind and anger diffusing nature at young age, then it will definitely sound strange. Let's end with, 'is it right, valid, acceptable to have warm blood at young stages? Is it wrong to have cool mind at any age?

Lesson 5
Discovering Myself

'Power Choice - Historical Achievements'

The nature and the universe have their own powers, forces and energies and runs on the same, but are molded, converted, designed and run by additionally fueled man's mind, moods, moves, nature and tastes. In other words, the powers, forces and energies of man are greater than that of the nature and of the universe.

No one can deny that the two worlds mentioned above are made/evolved or exist for man but not vice versa. Therefore, man brings all his forces into action and the resultant of such applications is the world we live in and experience.

Leaving here the earthly and space worlds that are basically puppets and subjective to man's dominance, let us move ahead to the powers of man that not only governs the nations and the world as a whole, but also controls each and every move of every existing man.

Hot and cold are those powers, violent and peaceful are in nature, unkind and kind in character, harming and harmless in results, selfish and selfless in methodologies, dictatorial and humble in projecting strength. The end products and the differences in gains through the same is what distinguishes the whole meaning and mood of the world.

Historical and spectacularly evident and revolutionary were the movements that swore tolerance and suffering their powerful weapons, even if needed to count the last breath as the precious token of peaceful milestones. We don't live for eternity here, but our history will certainly pitch its permanent tent.

Innovations and discoveries are our own, whereas influential, impactful, inspirational, guiding and leading are others' paths. Role models are they that not just ignite our spirits to follow them but are drivers to their destinies. It is you, the mood generator, that can gift others either tears or smiles, sobs or laughs. Choose...!

Weak man using strong powers of control is heavy and burdensome. It leaves stressful, strained and weary with little success or no success. Strong man using weak powers is meaningless exercise, only efforts but no results. Weak man using weak powers is equivalent to the strong man using weak powers. What we try to find and become here is, making of a strong man and handing over strong powers to the same, since we aim to master all that is in oneself and all that comes as force from others.

Wishing that you grasp the full knowledge of strong powers and full authority over them, which actually are contrast to the ones projected in this world and most commonly used by each and every one from infants to the old, learned to the unlearned, abled to the disabled, laymen to the saints, children to parents, students to teachers, common men to forces etc. to get going and get the things done. Discovering yourself, if becomes a joyful adventurous journey then mastering yourself will be smooth sail even in rough waters.

Lesson 6
Discovering Myself

'Subdue The Most Powerful – Dominate The Deadly'

A new moon night, a midnight emergency call, a compelling step to move out and walk a few miles, all alone, not so easy but essential. Pitch dark and absolute silence, no movements, no one around except for the stray dogs, alert with erect straight ears, dozens in number in each group at stone throw away distances. Trembling steps making loud noise signals the strays that the man is either scared, alien to that area, or have some wrong in mind.

Smart at zero decibel audacity, sharp at translating the foot sounds, one started barking low, another added little gain to its decibels, in no time all the dozens at distant places implemented their strategic plan not to allow even an inch movement. Mastering courage, a confident, bold voice exercising authority dominated those dozens of barks, advancing attacks, and all at once dropped ears down, moved back, some waged tails.

'Subdue them,' two words, very deep in reality, dominant in power, secret to survive, given to man in the genesis of human history by the maker of all that is in the world and worlds. If man fails to subdue the animal kind, and keep the wilds of the greens spreading into his dwelling territories, then his life would be no different from the trap inside the stray's circles and predators inside the bush which once was a clean field and a walkable path.

Not to be misunderstood here, man was on his way, dogs also on their duty. If those strays remain silent, and simply allow a stranger pass away, then it clearly indicates that none of them have the dog's qualities. They have lost the identifying sense, guarding capacity, and their original nature. If man cannot draw his inner right powers into action in suiting situations, then he is dead in senses, dummy at learnings, ignorant of the reactions/necessary measures to challenges and threats of life.

Noteworthy observation here is, man, if fails to be man, then all other forces will install themselves into dominant actions which is against the natural intent of all the worlds. Therefore, identifying himself as the main character in the entire universe, man must be on toes round the clock, investing his positive, constructive energies in dominance and expressing love by allowing the wilds to be in the forests, their dwellings, and the birds, the skies to soar, man in close relationships in family, neighborhood and societies.

Creating a world of your own, a favorable around you and a pleasant one to others, if becomes your motto, then peace, happiness and joy will be main moods and elements of the same. Be a good architect, great designer and generous gifter of noble worlds to the world!

Lesson 7
Discovering Myself

'Kids Not Cubs - Men Not Lions'

Waking on the road looking at the sky, standing near the fire in the absence of the mind, making business deals full of emotional feels, bringing anger forward before every talk, hiding all the ills while praying for the forgiveness, and allowing the ego still in charge while reconciling with the good friend, will lead you to the wrong destinies, wrong worlds, give wrong results and make all your efforts meaningless, but certainly cause accidents and loss; create strife, make hypocrite and label egoistic.

Drawing this parallel to wrong model, example, inspiration, and ideology or idol is a way to caution for the right focus while doing right thing. The reader you, could be an adolescent, teenager, young adult or old, must be having an understanding if not fully, at least to an extent, where you are heading, what you are becoming, what you are aiming and what you will be gaining.

For everything in the world to increase its measure, size and quantity, there's something called growth material, unless it is added to the former, nothing will grow/increase. Food is the growth material of man, animal, birds, plants and trees etc. Another brick, sand and cement are the increasing material of the walls, a drop of liquid with another etc. Foods basically are the only physical growth material meant for living beings, every species' feed is different, so is of man.

Man, though while taming wild beings, might be successful in disciplining them to get accustomed to his foods and habits, but animal can never become a human. Reverse of this could be possible and true, if he feeds himself on animal feed or brings up his kids on the beastly traits. Anger, retaliation, violence, jealousy, competitive nature, selfishness, mean mentality are such feeds that either we consume to appear fierce, powerful, reigning, rich or nurture our babies for the same.

Have we forgotten that we are raising kids not cubs, and we are men not lions? Discovering yourself opens the door for better understanding of being better and staying best. Feeding on good thoughts, cool lives, pleasant stories, nonviolent conversations, switching to different worlds when air turns hot and changes the atmosphere is the ideal step to have coolants of life. Wish, you keep some coolant always, at least in reserve, if not in action.

Lesson 8
Discovery Myself

'How Sweet - So Sweet - No Sweet'

Be it a color, be it a flower, a dish or a drink, a sound or a light, an ornament or an item, a car or a horse, a dance or music, everything establishes its distinct, honored, demanding, and dominant position on any occasion. Cultures and traditions of each land has its own registered way, method, material, practices and rituals.

Having set formats but with slight differences in taste and decorum, all occasions, functions and programs pitched their own ways of celebrations. Mangalsutras and garlands in the Indian culture, rings and bouquets in the western culture, sweets and cakes, coconut water and wine respectively, with a difference of accompanying Indian and western music, suiting dance moves etc. are distinct things but for one mood, happy.

It sounds truly sweet upon hearing someone say, 'how sweet are you!' A kind benevolent, a forgiver, a helping hand, a messenger of good news etc. are usually showered with praises prefixing or suffixing 'so sweet of you, so nice of you, so kind of you...!'

Sweetness, no doubt, has its unmovable position on every good, first, new, achievement, repeat of great memories and memorable happenings. Be it rich or poor, everywhere, sweet pops out from nowhere. And it is the sweet, on the sweet eve, for the sweet people and by the sweet, lovely near and dear.

Noteworthy here, though sweet is dominant but served and savored in little bites. Other dishes add up for a planned, nutritious menu. Too much of everything is harmful, loss making, and problem creative. Sweet tooth, sour buds, spicy blood appear bad in the pathological reports. When the readings are more/less than the required amount the advice follows with restrictions and additional curing agents. So, one might end up saying, 'no sweet please.'

As the pathological reports present what man has in his store (body) in excess/less, dangerous/harmful etc. So is the tongue, behavior, action and reaction, expose man's qualities in measure whether they are adequate/excess/less, most importantly of the nature, whether good or bad.

Therefore, to be a pleasing personality in one's surroundings, a peaceful being inside oneself, and a desired one by all, one must always strive to listen, 'how sweet, so sweet,' but never allow a day to say, 'no more please.'

Lesson 9
Discovering Myself

'Valid Expectations - Short Arm Donors'

Appearances mostly cheat and rarely demonstrate crystal clear. So, the common say, 'do not judge anyone/anything from outer appearance is flawlessly true and perfectly fitting, both in good and bad sense. We all play hide and seek, almost every day, every time and before everyone. Usually, the good qualities of man, though, he wishes to demonstrate, but the preoccupied impression against him in others doesn't let that happen.

Preoccupations could be on some personal bad experiences, could be based on others' experiences of the same, could be the result of the appearance or could be on right/wrong reporting. Bad qualities are never hidden by those who basically and openly project themselves as villainy kind of personalities. Dangerous are the willfully hidden bad in each and every one, like vipers that lurk in untraceable hideouts.

Expecting some gold or silver coins in alms during ancient times, a man at the temple entrance looked at the devotees going in to worship the divine one. But the devotees had a short arm that day, they ran out of all gold and silver. But looking at that lame man, they said, 'what you ask and need, we don't have. But what we have can suffice your need. We offer healing in the name of the Lord Jesus, receive it.

Expectations against some good must turn better, in case of a substitute but never worse, either when you run out of resources or have no heart of mercy. Give what others need, if you have, if not give them the needful, what you have. Something like the beneficiary at the temple gates was served with the needful.

Hiding the bad and appearing good is hypocrisy. And the hypocrisy is a continuous willful act accompanied by lies, false images, wrong claims, which in one word is cheating others always. Hypocrisy, unless converted into action against anyone is safe play, no harm to others, except the hypocrite moving closer to Oscar in daily acting.

Good people, though unrecognized can never be a threat. Bad people - visibly villainy, hypocritical - visibly good, are anytime equally or more harmful. A safe, healthy, and secure atmosphere is what the greatest expectation of everyone is. Are you a trustworthy or short armed here?

Lesson 10
Discovering Myself

'Tourist Heart - Discovery Mind'

Great is the brain of man which not just has unlimited expandable memory storage, but also is the master of every organ, every function of the same, and the only source on who the mind and heart are dependent. Mind and heart don't have any data of their own at all, they draw everything from the brain.

The former to think and decide, the latter to let the mind know how it feels upon its way of thinking and deciding. In fact, heart is the decider of decisions, but never to be forgotten, and be ever cautious that not all the signals, feelings, and state of the moment are right. Heart is always deceiving and it mostly works against the mind, against you. Therefore, it is right to say that, heart is man's own enemy.

Visiting places is one of the thrilling and exciting occasional events, either specifically planned, gifted as incentive, or upon someone's invitation etc. Touring is classified into two purposes and is attributed to two areas of our functioning, heart and mind.

The former, the heart takes man on a joy ride, resting mode from the yearlong hectic regular works and stressful life, all for fun, relaxation, and to see different worlds. The latter, the mind always looks to discover unknown, learn new things and put them in action for further part of life, such as industrial tour, study tour, business tours etc.

Let's take a tour of the heart before we end discovering myself topic. There are people living inside man, who we never see as people but emotions. Emotions, actually are the end products or expressions of heart's feelings which are displayed in various forms. Only few we name, like happy, sad, angry, irritated, frustrated, excited, jealous, hatred, moody, fussy etc.

Each feeling is a person in reality who could be one in the initial stages but many in the later development, when expressed. The final expression of the feeling is the strength gained upon a large army of joining together.

We will be discussing the same in detail in next lesson. Leaving you here with a question for now, what armies do you employ each day? What do they do for you? If you can discover an enemy inside you, then what are you going to do to eliminate the same?

Lesson 11
Discovering Enemy

'Immortal Army - Whispering Commander'

If there's any report of anyone who exists or existed in the human, divine, demonic and even in the animal and bird worlds, who has no enemy at all, then that report is either the biggest lie or that reporter had not travelled all those worlds. Since, it is impossible to find an enemy-less person or being, it is also impossible to find the same without battles, oppositions and challenges. It doesn't mean all mortal and immortal too have struggles, tensions, heartaches, difficulties, etc. they are exceptional.

Immortal divine is the Supreme, so has control over every being and everything. Mortal divine, learned able, having grip over all control systems too are free from the foresaid. Unlearned, control-less, ignorant of the powers and the weaknesses of such great powers feel entire life a burden, curse, battle, struggle, meaningless, impossible to handle etc. It doesn't stop there, they spend all their lives, worrying, troubled, wanting, weeping, tensed, frustrated, hopelessly exercising to kill those challenging, opposing, defeating and tormenting mighty powers of hell.

Pains, aches and burns, external and internal are the suffering part, every sick/deceased can feel, know to name and express them, but only the physician gets to know after hearing the patient, diagnosing and running tests accordingly, the reason and the way all that happened.

He/she also knows how to excite the suppressed cells and calm down the hyper acting, visible and micro cells of the body which are the effects of the presence of foreign material or the absence of healthy material, causing sickness, pain, swelling, disease etc. When the bodies agree to the physician's command through medicine, they gain back lost powers and stand tall like goliath after completing the full prescribed course.

Your attention must be caught here by the wonder working order of the commander in chief, the physician's war, one after the other through the pills, needles and rest to the patient, resulting the storm of worries, and war of sickening material surrendering and leaving the battlefield. A lion, a tiger, a bear, though chained around their necks, are not scared by the stick/rod of the ring master, but it is the confident vocal command of the latter that silences the wild beasts and limits them inside the allotted circles.

Your inner enemies, as discovered so far, anger, violence, hatred, temptation, depression, addiction, frustration etc. are immortal powers. They say, "we can't be killed, but very well be subdued by the learned, teachable and powerful cool people's whispering commands."

As we continue to rope in the nostrils of wild powers, you will be transformed to Miss/Mr. Cool soon. Till then keep exercising to have the right knowledge that can impart courage, strength and give command and authority over every power, which so far is out of your control and understanding.

Lesson 12
Discovering Enemy

'Carried Forward Stink - Brought Forward Scent'

Food, clothing and shelter for survival, dignity and protection, can be the only basic necessities all the human beings have in common. Not necessarily of the same kind, value and worth.

Some just eat to survive, wear to cover, and can even live under the open sky, beneath the trees. Some others adjust according to the given situation and feel content as long as they move from scarcity to surplus. The rest survive to eat and enjoy everything, they don't compromise in simple wear and dwelling.

Important here to bear in mind is, we all differ in categorizing the needs, comforts and luxuries. Those who are content with the fitting means of survival considers all others as extravagance and pleasuring spoilers against contentment. Nether will they strive to catch up with others in rest of possessions nor would like to consider them worth earning or gaining.

Those who endlessly race to have comforts, in no time will end up defining the luxuries as comfortable necessities. Moulding according to one's own interests can never become eternal definitions. It can be stated as redefining part of justifying oneself.

Returned from work, being out the whole day, a good shower with fragrant cleaning agents washes away the dirt, vanishes the stink, rejuvenates entire body, soul, detoxifies all fatigue, renews the energy chargers, making feel fresh, clean, light, scented, for the in-house next program in sequence.

Some do this before cuddling themselves between the sheets. Others, either don't bother about this or don't feel it's necessity, importance and benefits. They don't find much difference, and also loves to feel comfortable in dirt and odor. Such people might even carry forward unhealthy, untidy, bad practices for days and weeks.

Carrying forward the harmful weapons waged against one, some or many, before closing of the day is the casual, willful, regular practice of the offenders to load/sharpen for next round of attack. The sensitive at heart, compassionate, and kind never carries forward the willful/accidental offences but will extinguish the vengeful fire of the suffered, seeking forgiveness and cleanses conscience/spirit before the divine one.

Harsh, negative, attacking, hurting forces are enemies of all. They cannot be friends even one redefines and renames them. A noble person never carries forward anything bad but always tries to bring forward the good ones for self and for others.

It is the loss that is carried forward and the profit that is brought forward while making the balance sheet and sending them to closing and opening balances respectively. Assets and liabilities must always be tallied at the end of every closing year, which demonstrates every right and wrong financial move.

There is no option to keep the liabilities for longer period, as it represents bad handling of resources. There is no option again other than making greater profits and settling the losses.

Similarly, one must show improvement in all good qualities in order to reduce the stature of the bad ones. But thankfully, there is also another and best option to wipe off all bad by seeking forgiveness against whom the offence is made.

Making strong decision not to repeat the same and also having a heart to settle every account then and there never takes you to the situation where the previous wrongs are carried forward. Wishing that you leave behind every stink and carry forward the sweet scent that is pleasant to self and unto others.

Lesson 13
Discovering Enemy

'Traitors Of The Bosom - Invaders On The Side'

Identification and discerning are two prominent areas of life, if recognized well and detected perfectly, then naming them and dealing with them becomes very easy and effective. Identification relates with the known, whereas discerning is of the unknown, hidden, dark or mysterious. Identification, though many a times is pretty easy but dealing with each and every identified thing, issue, situation may not be that easy.

Discerning people, anticipating situations, predicting next moves may not be a possibility in every case and with every person, but an indication of all such next could be grasped with a constant careful watch and awakening spirit. To be advanced in such learning, one needs to spend a good amount of quality time with the past experiences as case studies. Time well spent and a thoroughly studied case can not only unravel the known, unknown and mysterious facts/reasons but also teaches care and caution to the future courses of actions.

Dealing with the topic discovering enemy, one must make sure, who the enemy is, where the same is, how, when and in what forms the enemy appears, works, deceives, confuses, damages, hurts, injures and destroys etc. Each and every one will be living with different kinds of enemies until they are marched on four shoulders to the grave.

They are, of the bosom - our most trusted, very own and the dearest, who might someday, sometimes or many a times can become betrayers. The invaders - who openly declares rivalry and attacks for the same. Dealing with the former requires caution, care, sensitiveness, diplomacy, love, understanding, tactics, and methods of control and transformation, because, they are our own and we can't lose them at any cost.

For the latter too the same methodology is in demand and at work, only if you really care for them to be won and make them a part of your own, otherwise, the very common and natural reaction is, each action/force demands equal and opposite reaction/force.

It is a never-ending battle, unless one surrenders, loses, gets destroyed. The next kind is hidden/open self, you. The first two kinds of enemies and the third kind, you, all together works only against you. You are the attacker, the attacked, but the suffered in all ways.

Mastering myself doesn't teach same reactions in opposite force, but opposite forces in diffusing manner. But to go there, you must be an expert in identification and discernment. So, making peace with self, loving betrayers and winning invaders, if becomes your mission, then your victory over mission impossible becomes a flying banner.

Lesson 14
Discovering Enemy

'A Tool And A Weapon - No One's Friend'

A thought being so wonderful, excellent, powerful, revolutionary, table turner, fiery, mind blowing, etc. as long as remains inside one's own brain is purely nonexistent, non-effective and lifeless. In order to give it the needed power, strength, force, working capability, one must release it either in sound, script, picture or expression form.

Unless at least one of these forms are attached to the thought form, nothing, absolutely nothing will happen in the external visible real world, but so many things can happen inside oneself. If those thoughts are good, happy, helpful, charitable, etc. then he/she will be rejoicing, dancing, singing, flying in the skies by attaching happy emotions to happy thoughts inside himself/herself.

If the same thoughts are attached to expressions, then they will be visible to the outer world, but even then, the enjoyment limits to solo participant. If those thoughts have something to do with anger, irritation, frustration, jealousy, hatred, quarrelsome, enmity, vengeful, insult etc. but are never projected outside, then he/she will be led to high or low pressures of blood, resulting in health issues both for short and long terms.

If those thoughts are concerned about self and are taking bad, ugly, disliking, hateful, cussing etc. forms, then his/her inner world will be full of self-destructive powers which could lead to harsh steps against own, including hurting and suicide. But if those thoughts are having bad, dirty, ugly, romantic, cinematic, lustful, sexual feelings against the opposite gender, then the inner world of those thought producers will not only be filled totally with filth, but also disrespect against each and every one.

All these seems to be safe as long as they remain inside one's mind, but if these thoughts are not tied strong to the control string, then one day they will rush out like a wind storm or whirlwind, shake and burst like an earthquake and a volcano, or gush out like flood waters crossing over or breaking off the dam gates.

A knife in the chef's kit, a chisel with the carver, a sickle in the harvester's hands is a beautiful, good tool as long as they are used for the designed purposes. None of those are meant to convert into weapon form, to attack and kill anyone. No household exists without a kitchen knife, so is no house attracted to penal code of conduct for possessing the same, because they are under lawful usage, tool not weapon.

As learnt above, expressions of emotions are harmless and don't attract any dispute, punishment as long as they are working wonders inside one's own mind, but are dangerous to self and may be at the verge of slipping into outer world that might turn into offence.

Therefore, it is better to destroy all ill thoughts and give working capacity to all good thoughts. Remember, a knife in lawful usage is friendly tool of all but in unlawful manner is no one's friend. May you possess good tools always and have control power over every inward and outward thought!

Lesson 15
Discovering Enemy

'Sorry - No Sorry'

Coming to the end of the topic discovering enemy, let us go through the straight check list and find out what all areas of life do one need to spend time in undoing all the checked boxes. But before giving you that list, you must be made aware of kinds of people who are categorized into various groups to see where do you stand among them.

The first kind is, those who always work for constant improvement and seek any kind of guidance to achieve. There are others who finds the need for improvement but never show submissiveness under any guidance, but stand self-learners. The second is, those who think they know everything and they are perfect. So, they neither accept their faults nor allow anyone to correct them. The third kind is, those who are completely ignorant of the knowledge of any improvement or such areas of improvement. Those under the third type again have teachable and unteachable kinds.

The last group is, though having known about any such area of improving, refining and educating self, but still are least bothered to spend their time, energy, money and other resources etc. on the same. This kind of group is, eat, drink and make merry, we are least bothered where the rest of the world goes.

The list here begins, but appears to be endless. May or may not you need everything, but as you begin to scan down you will feel the importance to undergo this moulding man series, mastering myself. The major expressions of inner feelings and outer provoking which we would be dealing are:

Anger, ego, depression, moods, powers, pressures, pride, frustration, hatred, defeat, insult, sadness, hurt, jealousy, violence, irritating, sulking, bad, dirty, ugly, ill/filthy feelings, intolerance, abuse, lies, cheat, deception, betrayal, rejection, negligence, unwanted, uncared, unloved, unfaithfulness, loss of finance, job, dear ones, wealth, health, joy, peace, happiness etc. Apart from these, we need to check whether we possess and express human, beastly, demonic or divine feelings, emotions and expressions.

You will be asked here to spend little time observing the beastly and demonic actions and reactions. And also, whether they are in any ways different from human and divine. If so, shouldn't you be asked to remain there little more and fill in your mind and memory with the same and point out the differences? This will help you to check before or after you express any emotion or feeling, and differentiate whether they are of human, beastly, demonic or divine.

A regular check after hurting, hitting, attacking, troubling, paining others will make you realize and reduce the power, force and strength of negative destructive acts. All these will only work, if and only if, you fall into first category and have a heart to say sorry. But if you possess an ego, self-esteemed, prideful heart, then saying sorry would be next to death to you. You might say, 'sorry, no sorry,' but never, 'I am sorry.' For such, even heavens will say, 'we are sorry' Miss/Mr. Unteachable!

Lesson 16
Knowing Real Enemy

'Front Line Soldier - Vested Interests'

Anointed king has very less days and moments to truly enjoy his life, if at all he is a concerned one of his people. This can be possible and true in case of an uncaring, reckless and an irresponsible one.

The caring king spends all his days of supremacy in trying to create peace and harmony in his kingdom, security in all the surrounding borders attached to neighboring nations. The success of both the initiations will gift a wonderful life with all abundance, both for the people and for the king. If either of the two takes desired shape, then the other might become a serious headache.

The bigger the kingdom, the greater the challenges and efforts. It is difficult to satisfy everyone. It is impossible to keep everyone happy. It can be a beautiful dream to remain a respected, loved, honored and accepted king of all, for that making moves to be the same must stand one's primary motto and foremost priority.

The king is only the face of the kingdom, whereas the rest of his people are the main body. The face is the display monitor, whereas the whole body is the working unit. In any case, the face must be saved from all insults and shame.

Good people are the king's major contributors in nation building, supportive pillars of its strength, glorifying image of its pride, backbone of its rule, breath of its sustenance. Bad natured people are like moth, pests, rust, rodents, bacteria and viruses, which invisibly, unnoticeably reduces the strength to shattering weaknesses. The percentage of good and bad forces at work if measured on a scale as 60 and 40, or 70 and 30, then it can be a secure, happy and smooth functioning one. If the reverse of the numbers is nation's mood, then the king/ruler will be pressurized and becomes the main sufferer.

In democracy, people vote and crown their leader for two reasons, one, by good people with good intentions, to gain good results and to have a good life. The other, who wishes to get their vested interests and for that either opts quietly to be a passive supporter or becomes a direct player.

Our body is a composition of hundreds of major and minor organs and parts. So is our brain, mind, heart, and spirit/conscience a combination of millions of major, minor and minute thoughts, feelings, emotions and expressions.

But only two are projected outwardly resulting upon two categories of reactions, they are either anger or smile. A smile on the face is the captain who goes for the toss and so is the anger. The one who wins the toss projects the expression.

Smile and anger cannot play together. Though, sometimes a smile is brought immediately after demonstrating anger, it is not simultaneous, but one after the other. The reverse of the same is also possible.

A crowned gentleman/lady must always introspect, whether the anger, which is always at display is the result of vested interests of internal/external forces, making it front line soldier or voluntary choice. In any case, if the same decides to make smile the face of life, then anger must be defeated at every toss. We will do it as we make a constant march towards enemy's camp, negative forces, slowly and steadily.

Lesson 17
Knowing Real Enemy

'Determined Leader - Forced Follower'

Learning to drive a vehicle, to ride a horse, to fly a plane, to sail a ship etc. is a mere ability to operate a machine or control a being. It can help you to take a faster, easy and comfortable journey. The means of transportation can also accommodate at least one more person other than the rider, driver, sailor and pilot along with their goods too. But to proceed on a journey determined, one must have complete knowledge of the destination and of the route.

It makes the traveler's work easy and carries to the destined location without being lost. But reading the signals en route is too complicated when switched to strange lands, new waters or unknown skies. No doubt, all the signals universally symbolize one and same, but entering and exiting the interconnecting routes needs sharp and undivided attention along with thorough knowledge.

It is where the destination is missed and gets lost into unplanned, unwanted, undesired and unnecessary worlds. Though, we keep roaming in the strange beautiful, amazing, wonderful, lovely, cool, pleasant, and marvelous world, but feel restless at certain point and wish to hit onto the exit route immediately, because we missed our dwelling, resting, purposed and our very own heaven.

Taking a U-turn requires to pass by again the same route until we reach the right spot where we got lost. Drawing this as a parallel to life's journey, an effort is made to make you understand that rectifying or correcting wrong steps is undoing everything that went wrong just like passing back through all the wrong stations headed.

Missing the mark not just happens by misreading, but also by misleading or misguiding too. In any case, coming back is the needful step to undo wrong journey. As learnt in the previous part that there are only two major expressions of major emotions and their reactions, smile and anger, we are heading to see if the expresser is a determined leader or a forced follower, purposefully missed or mislead.

Anger is the most common expression of every feeling, thought, happening, situation, etc. which goes against our way. But mostly, majority of the angry people makes it their way of choice and they feel nothing wrong, instead very comfortable.

They demonstrate this reaction for even petty things, against anybody and everybody, irrespective of any age, gender, relation, status etc. As lenders cannot do much against willful defaulters other than making every possible recovery attempt, so is any teaching a hopeful attempt to rope in control string in the nostrils.

Respecting the other person and his/her feelings is the primary step to control anger. One must know that everyone has his/her values and worth, no one has the right to put them down, demean, disrespect and hurt. You are an angry person; it doesn't warrant you to express as you wish.

Every wrong expression attracts in-house, departmental, penal disciplinary actions. One must see to refrain from all these. So, start respecting others as you respect yourself. Take initial step to pour coolant in your hot machine, your brain and mind to head on a cool journey.

Lesson 18
Knowing Real Enemy

'Evident Void - Vacuum Filling'

No one is a master of any subject, topic, art, craft, skill, work even language etc. right from the birth or young age. In order to learn up to adequate levels, one doesn't require much of training, time and efforts. But to be advanced, expert and mastering levels, one must be committed, dedicated, by possessing special abilities of observation, reason, research, discovery and innovation.

Any of the above said can be a handy tool and mastery art even without any particular teaching and training, if the learner has learning and observing ability. Our world is full of millions, billions, trillions.... and googolplexes of things. Even in our surroundings there exist thousands of different things.

Naming everything and having known about the same is not a kids play. But it is very essential to possess right knowledge and information about the things, works, worlds, beings; whether human, divine, animal and demonic associated with us.

Possessing the knowledge is an extraordinary ability, while stating or expressing the same perfectly is a marvelous art.

Heard of a half full or half empty glass? A glass having liquid up to half level is seen by a school of empty/ unsatisfied/ complaining thoughts as half empty, and by the school of filling/satisfied/content as half full. The former and the latter though appears to be right in their observations and declarations, but both are looking at the other half and the former just states that he/she can see the emptiness and points out to the fillers that it is your duty, you did only half work, half is still unattended. The latter wants the emptiness turn into fullness either on their own or upon pointing out by someone.

Looking at the trench to erect a tall building, the architect knows what material suits better and fitting that can withhold it stable, strong, and long-lasting. Sometimes, we do feel hallow or emptiness in our lives, everything seems to be void and vacuum. The natural reaction for this is depression, frustration, irritation and anger. Though, the first three make their appearance but the last one, anger projection will be intense and fierce.

Sitting back and moving to the origins of vacuum filled life unravels reason, at the same time filling the void with needful fitting material eases the mood and changes the temperament. The cause of the vacuum could be due to some loss, fight, insult, fears, phobias or insecurities of life. Being lost in the same mood and temperament for long is like filling the vacuum in the evident void.

Stop being sad, sorry, regretful for what you can't do anything now, rather rise up, refresh, rejuvenate yourself, shake off all ill feelings and cool down your anger.

Lesson 19
Knowing Real Enemy

'Indigestible Appetite - Delhi-Belly Treat'

Choosing from any two is not a big deal or tough task, if the differences are vast. But it certainly needs right sense and thorough knowledge when the differences are almost similar and narrow. Though, a choice in the latter doesn't result much loss, if at all it goes wrong, but is definitely very big in case of the former.

When the options get increased to greater numbers, then the time required to finalize a selection too takes a lot. Staring through the articles and price list at Expo, the desires and wishes demands wings but the budget quickly jumps in to clip off all the big flying feathers on the wings. Heart shrinks down to actual size of the spending capacity and looks pale at the short armed unfulfilled desires that are wanting to stretch and reach the happiness which is staring back from the other bay, way far.

Imagine yourself at a wedding banquet, unsure about the choice of unknown cuisine, moving to-and-fro holding a plate at the display buffet, finally got the plate filled, either serving self or with the staff's help. You can't enjoy anything that is strange or new to you. You could even end up suffering Delhi-belly.

Imagine yourself again at the same place of your favorite cuisine, your appetite demands for more and more. Blame the taste buds, the chef or even your craving intestines, the feasting enjoyment was momentary resulting indigestion and/or dysentery. Saying no is the hardest work, but the biggest secret for a happy, easy and comfortable life. Learn to say no to things unknown, learn to learn about things unknown and say no if it/they doesn't suit you, learn to say no to known, favorite things if got in excess or offered again and again.

The factors resulting in angry expressions are like foods on the buffet, some known and some unknown, some favorite and some allergic. They are also like the articles at the Expo display, expensive, beyond reach but wanted and desired.

Too little of the desired, too much of the loved, nothing of the wanting creates unsatisfactory, fatigue and frustrating feelings respectively. Preparing your heart to be content, suiting the budget, capable to the digestive system, avoids all kinds of scarce, poverty and sickening feelings. Eat healthy live healthy, think well be happy, say no, stay safe.

Having learnt that the anger is man's enemy, but need to know now that the factors that lead to angry expressions are anger's real enemies. Hope, you have come to know that it is the innocent victim, anger, that always get caught, and it is also the helpless man who is pressurized to pose angry expression with yelling/screaming voice, accompanying frightening and threatening tone, gets the bad image. But the real culprits are anger producing factors, which enjoy unsuspecting, unnoticeable and scot-free roam.

Lesson 20
Exposing Enemy -Safeguarding Anger

'Overloaded Back - Aching Muscles, Pulling Nerves'

Having precious things, vulnerable to theft, pests and rodents, putting the fence, spraying the preventive, laying the trap are necessary and right moves of safeguarding before facing any loss or damage. In spite of all these, if the trespasser still makes to move in, then the next step is to catch hold and expose for proper treatment.

It might sound strange, but evidently correct that, many a times, the trespassers, offenders, are either our very own, close or known to us. On being caught in such cases, the exposure and treatment differs totally opposite, because they are our dear ones, who we can't afford to lose.

It might differ from the foresaid when we don't care of the loss and consequences. When our own trespass against us and trespass against others, we naturally tend to protect them first and later take any corrective or punishing measures. If that is somebody else, then the only first option seems to be catching hold, exposing and punishing.

Overloaded backs, climbing up and down the stairs, working long hours usually and very naturally will lead to aching back, muscles, and pulling nerves. This will cause sleeplessness, which additionally result in side effects, such as headache, stress, strain, tension and restlessness.

All these very obviously will make way and push anger forward. Anger being under these pressures don't know much other than responding to each and every word, move and approach of others in irritating, quarrelsome and fighting modes.

Same is with every kind of work, whether physical or mental. Anything overloaded, overworked and/or over thought could lead to same consequences. We must bear in mind that anger has no choice, no control, no measure of its own.

It is man who has the control system, and it is he who decides the way of expressing anger, the amount of quantity, force, and the kind of quality.

Expecting anger to be in one's control is then an absolute wrong way of mastering oneself. Teaching the mind to remain cool under every pressure, to ignore all aches, pains and stresses and training all the muscles and nerves to stand submissive to the commands of mind is the only effective and right way to safeguard anger from being pushed forward.

As seen above, when the offenders or wrong doers are our own, we generally try to hide them from being caught, exposed and punished. Likewise, we must consider all our overly troubled bodies, mind and their side effects as our own and need to be safeguard them from being exposed. Anger must be respected and given due honor.

We will be learning more in next lesson. But for today, we will be deciding to spend some time with the things that lead to stress, strain, headaches, sleeplessness etc., which relatively leads to unwanted, unnecessary and bad anger. A question before saying bye for now, what kind of anger you project, good or bad, necessary or unnecessary, profitable or loss making? Think till we meet in next lesson.

Lesson 21
Exposing Enemy - Safeguarding Anger

'Anger's Demand - Respect Me, Be Honored'

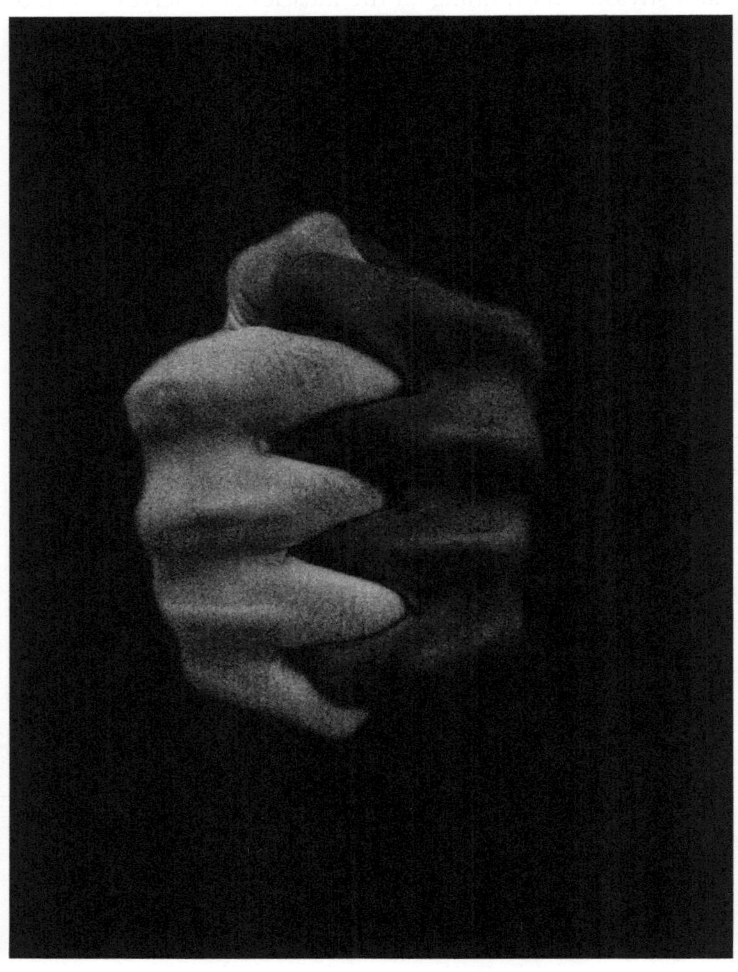

All glory is mine.' This is the endless and tireless race of mankind, whether eligible or ineligible, real or fake, earned or stolen, deserving or demanded, but it should be mine and I must be glorified. Glorification, undoubtedly comes pretty expensive, if at all one thrives it to be one's crown, unfading. It also involves violent force into action by the strong headed, muscle powered and wealth exhibitionists. Kind hearted, soft natured, humble souls, young and the old, rich and the poor, literate and illiterate, friends and foes, near and dears, everyone says, it's my pride, your envy.

Passing through the evident and undisclosed areas of the lives of thousands and millions, the claimants of humility, unglorified, cool and calm practitioners and exhibitionists, unhesitatingly the acknowledgement makes way to Jesus Christ, the Messiah of mankind, who never wished to be glorified and in turn gave it to the deserving and worthy. While the scriptures states, when people approached for healing and received the same, He credited their faith, glorified the Father in heaven and wished to pocket nothing for himself.

It would be unjust if the incident of Christ being angry doesn't make room to be mentioned here, the only incident recorded of His life, while He was cleansing the temple, preparing for the Passover, which was turned into market place by the actual custodians. But His love and forgiveness against all those who accused Him of blasphemy and sedition, ran the whip on his back, mocked and nailed Him to death surpassed the harmless anger projected at the temple, saying, "Father, forgive them for they not know, what they do."

The most important point to be emphasized here is, it is the anger of the people that chained Him, dragged to the courts for continuous and emergency midnight hearings, presented before the high priest, Herod the great, king of Judea and before Pontius Pilate, the then governor of Judea thrice and finally sentenced to thirty-nine stripes and death on the cross. His history today chrysographed as "Prince of Peace."

Books of the mortals and of the immortals, good and bad, peaceful and violent, loving and envying, all have certain amount of anger disciplining and punishing, harmless and harming, human and beastly, divine and demonic. The grip over anger is not as easy as control over clutch, accelerator and brake under the feet.

It doesn't come under anyone's authority before writing volumes of dishonoring, disrespecting, demeaning and destroying estates, empires, relations and breaking hundreds of hearts. But it can be avoided if one learns to respect the anger and doesn't bring it forward for every petty, unnecessary and unwanted issue but speaks wise, deals cleverly, solves tactfully and settles diligently.

The successful application of the foresaid never makes room for anger to take the stage and play ugly role that dishonors and demeans everything. Experiences from the past, exercises of the present become our today's glorious crown and tomorrow's chrysography. Honor anger, it has such a great value, which is way beyond than your own worth.

Lesson 22
Exposing Enemy - Safeguarding Anger

'Demand-Less Production - Demanding Warehouses'

Workers in the factory possess no knowledge about the supply and demand in the market, other than assuming that, since there is a demand for more production, the supply too is more and the consumption/usage is no doubt in excess. It also gives the impression that the product they make is fitting to the choice of the consumer. The situation and fact could be opposite and totally different from the worker's assumption, but they have nothing to do with it. It is the look out of the supply and the marketing team.

There were, are and will be numerous instances when the liaison among the production, distribution and marketing personnel standout of coordination and cooperation, the resultant was, is and will be demand for more warehouses. Thoughtless production, wrong distribution, and poorly marketed products lead to the shutdown of so many units, factories and industries.

Creating more space for warehouse is not the solution, rather the remedy and the right way to correct previous wrongs is, stop production immediately. Secondly, monitor the market until the goods make a smooth move resulting empty store houses. And again, if this is not done at the right time, then this perfect remedial later would prove ineffective, which is loss over loss.

Comparing with the above said, many of us overly produce anger, irrespective of the need and usage. What better can this product be for us if we don't know how to destroy or diffuse it? Isn't it similar to the overly packed warehouses? Anger, as long as remains inside the production and storage units, appears intangible to both and to others. The moment it is expressed, it's tangibility and its effect will be clearly evident.

Travelling back to our initial learnings about diffusers, we must always bear in mind to carry them. Good diffusers act like perfect shock absorbers. It's a no joy ride without them. Learning to produce the required amount, using it in a proper sense defines the levels of understanding and maturity.

Heard of, 'anger is man's enemy'? Does the above picture say so or quite opposite to it? 'Exposing the enemy - safeguarding anger' doesn't spare anyone, it is crystal clear in observations, vocal in its declaration and impartial even unto its master. If not, it would be unjust and unfair unto it.

Man, always plays blame game and pictures himself clean and feels safe, throwing the dirt on situations, surroundings, circumstances, and bad emotions. Correcting ourselves again here that, there's no emotion that is good or bad, but the situations and happenings which produce feelings accordingly and expressed in good or bad taste.

Therefore, man must own the complete responsibility of birthing bad expressions like anger, strife, temperament etc. his hold on every hurting, insulting, envious and troubling moods, when not released well and allowing all the failing moves and pushing anger forward. So far, you were asking anger to be in your control and allowed it to pass several trainings and treatments unnecessary, but today, it says, control yourself and don't push me for your defense over your silly, meaningless, worthless wrongs. Will you listen to me?

Lesson 23
Spectacular Me -Blind You

'Serpent's Eyes - Dangerous Boost'

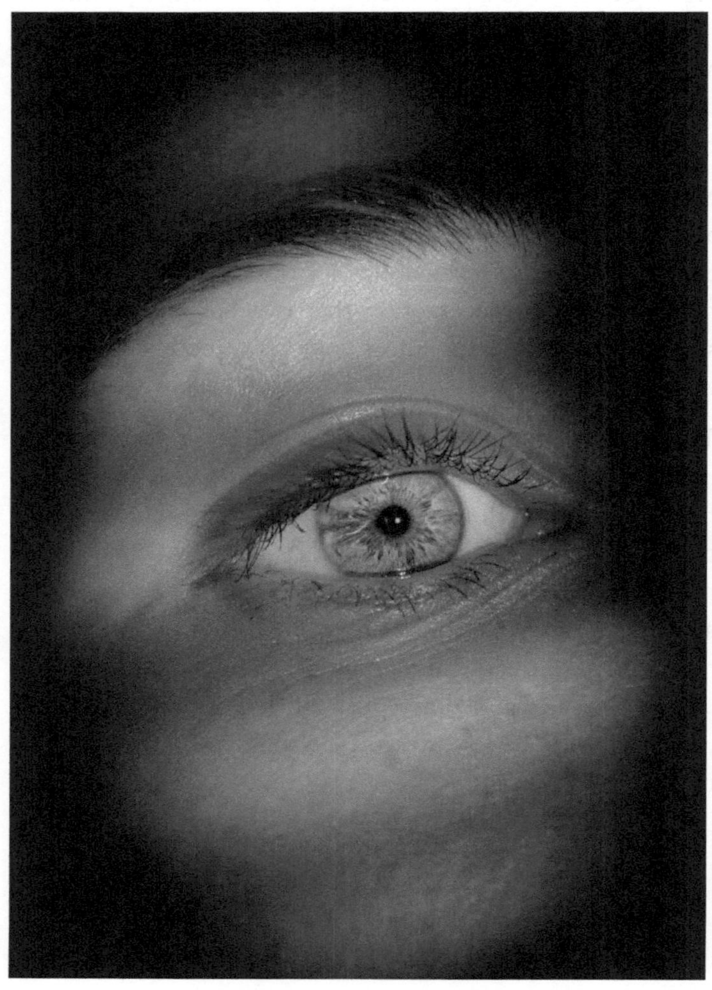

Concern is not a commonly and easily found element in all the human beings, unto others. But for self and the one related to that same self, it is evidently and spectacularly visible in each and everyone. Concern for others possesses, kind, charitable, compassionate, merciful and sacrificial positive selfless attributes.

It keeps others in front and does everything favoring in their interests. They think, act and react keeping the idea of others' feelings, benefits and well-being at the center of every walk and talk. They distance themselves from listening to any advice that has even a minute presence of compromise on the principles.

The one contrary to these has a greater concern that revolves around self and his/her world. The concern here has a conscious, watchful, cleverly, mean and deceitful attribute with me, mine and my focus.

A serpent is known for craftiness and cleverness. It is very attentive and sharp in being watchful, escaping and swift in attacking. But the presence of it near human vicinities cannot go unnoticed easily. Though, it makes clever and crafty moves, it can be foolishly got caught.

This is something similar to a train passing over the river bridge, the passengers in the front coaches feel that the train had crossed over as soon as those coaches exit the bridge, but behind are several coaches making it long still running over the bridge.

The snake too moves ahead with its head and eyes unnoticeably crossing over the enemy's radars, but the long body up to the tail is blind to it and is clearly visible to all. The snake though is said to have greater vision, actually possess very poor eye sight. It can sense very well but can't see properly. It is indeed very efficient against sensing dangers because it has an additional strength to boost its eye sight on being under attack.

Man, who claims to be having clear sight, fore sight and long sight actually lives with various kinds of blindness all through his life. His life consists of dark side and blind side, which again, a major portion could be unknown to him till he leaves this world.

This has several reasons like, being ignorant, being told but ignored, having no knowledge, deliberate and foolish unto correction etc. Concern of self as being the point of focus here, and the major issue is with those who are self-concerned and the troubles they create for others.

A serpent being naturally poor at sight, but is completely blind upon hatching eggs. It gets even all its young ones devoured. Only the fortunate gets an escape to life from parent cannibal.

Man being blind in anger too devours many like the serpent. The fortunate ones make an escape, the strong ones wage a war, the mighty ones get the upper hand. Finding someone without having anger is next to impossible, but finding a bit of concern unto others in angry people can make wonder working difference.

Lesson 24
Spectacular Me - Blind You

'Guilty Powers - Developing Tools'

Slavery, who said it had been completely eradicated, it is no more an extant of the 21st century? Such declarations and statements make way to pitch their tents as universal observations only with ignorant mind and blind eye. It is broadly and only a valid partial truth in the sense of nations being independently free and republic.

Fight against slavery has taken centuries and millenniums in various parts of the world, but still is powerfully dominant, except for giving the world nations their individual name, identity, flag and geographical land. Can anyone dare to prove and show a land that is completely free from enslaving state and slavery mindset? Slavery cannot enter the books of extinct unless the weak volunteers to walkout from serving the powerful. If that was so easy, millenniums in ages and millions of struggles wouldn't have earned space in thousands upon thousands of history books.

Call it the powerful suppressing the powerless or the weak volunteering under the shadow of mighty one's umbrellas, the existence and extant of slavery will remain until the last person on the earth kicks the bucket to enter the books of nonexistent. Opting for slavery with harsh treatments is no one's desired choice as a bread winning source, but the curse of illiteracy, ignorance, laziness and spinelessness to fight against the injustice meted out.

Sweet blackmail of the crafty, blinding the needy with little perks still makes someone a king, others rulers, ministers, authorities, bosses and masters. Such people create national, provincial, occupational, industrial and professional slaveries. After taking a broader view of greater slavery, we come to the other end of the funnel, a narrow one, domestic slavery. Blessed are the homes and the people who see enslaving treatment at home as totally extinct.

Upper hand not necessarily holds authoritative stand always, it is the sternness of an individual which emboldens the loud vocals wavery free. Dealing with anger as our primary subject, it is important to have a bird's eye before peeping inside the microscopical lens. In some instances, it is not the head of the family, whose anger or authority has obedient reaction but the unruly, wild, tempered and disobedient children's. But most of the cases, it is the head of the family who is unknown of right expressions, has wild temper, untamed emotions present all the mad angles of anger.

A family order, obedience, submissive system, a bond, a relation has lovely values that keeps everyone together and shapes into fine characters with learnings, experiences, trials and errors etc. As each day passes over us, we do pass through many things in life and all that passed away remains only mere history and experience.

Wise children consider parent's anger, could be harsh, fierce and wild but a course correction. No pain is felt looking back at years and decades, but gives only thankfulness for a successful, well positioned and well-established life. Parents might spend guilty moments, days, years and also decades for being such main characters of mad angles cinematic life, but the disciplined child see it a developing tool. What do you see today, guilty power or developing tool?

Lesson 25
Spectacular Me - Blind You

'Controlling Commands - Managing Orders'

Digitalization has projected patience for decades and was content with baby steps. Man could not notice when and how it developed its pace, uncatchable, unstoppable, and uncontrollable. It has an enormous amount of positive side but a little, almost negligent amount of negative side, which is actually sufficient to make him a dummy.

It might sound foolish, rubbish and insane, but prophetically and analytically a foretold state of mind that man has stepped into and will be advancing soon with an unnoticeable and dangerous speed. Since, man has entered into the world of commands and controls, digital, he has very less to do with his senses, mind, heart, emotions and feelings. The advancing world neither would be a creative nor innovative but a derivative.

Need for millions and billions of minds, muscles and hearts were required for works involving creative and innovation, but the world of derivatives is a small working class, almost a five to ten percent of the existent world's population. All that has to do tomorrow is organizing, managing and adjusting, which only involves digital commands and controls. What better has the rest ninety to ninety five percent to do other than going nuts, mad and insane?

Heard that, "an idle man's mind is devil's workshop." Imagine the world with five hundred and fifty plus billions of insane minds, the devil's workshop! It's scary, fearsome, horrific and traumatic! Wait, this is not the end, but the beginning of another era, which the insane population would be initiating and fighting back to reverse the order and get back what was snatched away from them. This is not a thumb/finger play on the smart screen or mouse click on the monitor, rather a revolutionary war against the powerfully equipped, digitally secured, mightily protected and Legionized individuals, companies, institutions and hosts of atomic and nuclear escorts.

The question is, is it possible? If at all the former analysis, prediction or logic is believable, then the need for a war against it is certain. Therefore, the possibility of triumph over it cannot be uncertain, impossible or unimaginable, but a reality like many revolutions.

Since, man is going to be replaced by digitalization, he will be left to dummy state, and then his only state of mind, feelings, emotions would be majorly anger, irritation, frustration, powerlessness and hopelessness. We would be dealing with scores of negative forces, means and methods of fighting them, maintaining cool and strong even until a single ray of hope is just remaining alive, which would be our fighting and winning ray, but all this in our second part of Mastering Myself.

Hoping that you had a great journey so far, have understood very well about yourself, your enemies, your helpers, the need to realize, the necessity to awaken, educate and change yourself, wishing paradigm shift in your transitional process and a mastering command over yourself as we conclude the first part of Mastering Myself!

PART 2

Lesson 1
Understanding Emotions - Wise Handling

You never know them until you spend time with inquisitive, curious, listening, learning and accepting heart; anyone, anything, a truth, myth, fairy tale or a fact.

You never know their positive and negative sides, their strengths and weaknesses, they are friends or foes, unless you have an experience, training, teaching, reporting or idea about them.

You never know what makes you strong or weak, what makes you or breaks you, what proves you or disproves you, until you peep in inside of you, introspect there and understand yourself.

You never know what you are and can never be unless you allow to keep your powers and strengths at work.

You never know your worth until you realize, someone says to you, you achieve big or make something innovative, extraordinary or you lose the same.

You never know is an endless list.

Therefore, this series of **Mastering Myself Part Two** is an initiation to enlighten the unknown you, your abilities, powers, strengths, your enemies and weaknesses, to empower you with full armor and to equip you with complete understanding of handling almost each and every emotion, a step by step move for triumph and victorious self.

What follows from here will be case studies, illustrations, stories and poems, and each part will have a case, observation, learning and application accompanying few questions.

Beginning with zealous and jealous, where only the first letter and little pronunciation is different in both, the former focuses on the positive unknown, whereas the latter revolves around the negative side, wanting to be greater, better, fairer, richer, stronger, cleverer than others.

It has a positive side to become the foresaid, but negative side of disliking, hating, demeaning, degrading, insulting and envying nature against all others. This leads to hypocrisy, cheat, deceit and competitive way of living. All these only makes path for sulking and nagging mode of living.

Therefore, being zealous to move ahead in learning good, doing good and living good, if becomes our only aim and agenda of life, then we are at the first successful steps of killing all negatives that makes moves for wrong ways, wrongs thoughts, wrong actions, wrong life, wrong image and wrong character.

The former intention creates volumes of pages in good history, whereas the latter has good amount of material, strong but all with bad reporting.

What better it is, after living decades of life worth nothing?

What better it is, running behind others and feeling complete life bad about self and wishing worse for them?

What better it is, achieving so many awards for excellence in various fields but having destroyed all that same with bad temper, loose talk and mad reactions?

What better it is, having so many degrees but lack commands and controls over self?

What better it is, spending thousands and millions in external beautification and internal transformation that has a repute needing constant makeover, which is bad, worse and ugly at heart?

What better it is, after all, having lived a king size life but without legacy that has no good content to carry forward?

What better it is, if you have no answers for these?

Think! Think good, think big, think well, think great and wish others a good, better, best, great, happy, successful, complete mastery life, and they will boomerang you!

Wish and pray that may your life be filled with good boomerangs full of blessings!

Lesson 2
Handling Pressure

A genius and another genius, neck to neck in all races, academic, extracurricular and even at every sport and game. The topper aims to always remain there, whereas the second ranker always want to climb to the top.

Has anyone seen success or failure unaccompanied by praises or criticisms? Had it ever happened that success wants to make silent march out of the grounds, auditoriums, result centers and through the streets, bazaars and markets? Has humility succeeded so well that any triumph goes dumb and simply avoids processions? It is neither impossible to find nor difficult to see such celebration less victories, but pretty rare. Since, achievements are loud, so are celebrations grand and processions large.

Years passed by, the same tough competition continued with the topper securing high numbers, points and grades. The second ranker, after repeated trials, harsh pressures from parents, peers, pet teachers began to see the decline in the progress chart, unable to bear the brunt, slipped into silent, unresponsive mode.

Ultimately, muteness overpowered, and lead to depression, but not before loading, experiencing and exhibiting enormous amount of jealousy. Undisclosed was the root cause for this gradual downfall until several sittings at counseling centers and shelling out nearly millions of bucks.

What went wrong, that a full life, packed with tons and loads of intellectual capacity suddenly gone dumb? Where did all those energies, strengths, capabilities, intelligence, knowledge, wisdom, confidence, boldness, creativity, skills and talents go? What will happen to this just missed genius? Is there a way to overcome?

"The Genius and just missed genius," this is how the slogan goes after every result declaration. The topper is known as The Genius and the runner up just missed genius. Initially, it was OK as long as innocence was ruling over the life and never ever the pressure was felt, though it was mounted right from the infancy.

The pressure angles usually begin with comparisons and with targeted goals. Parents have a common and natural tendency to point out someone and ask their child to compete with the same and prove better than her/him in all areas, starting from academic marks to career, earnings and possessions.

Isn't it better to show the 100 number, maximum marks and ask your child to meet it perfectly? It's not someone in the class, family or neighborhood our target goal to meet or cross, but studying smart, performing well in exams and securing cent percent marks.

What if the child misses few marks out of hundred and/or lesser than the targeted people's marks? How soft and how harsh can we be against this missed goal? Up to an extent of making the child realize the importance and need to be get full numbers, or hitting hard verbally or physically to an extent that the child begins to feel bad about himself/herself or jealous about others and slip into sulking and depressing state?

What best do you do as a parent under such pressure to see your child at the top ranks? What best as a student or child or an adult you see to handle your pressure?

Lesson 3
Judging Pressures

A balloon, a football, a rubber tube inside a car, bus, truck's tyre, aerated water and soda is good for nothing, if there's is no adequate amount of pressure in them. Imagine this globe without air pressure and also with excess of the same.

Think of a voyage without hind pressure and with too much of opposite winds. Recollect your experiences of one or more of these that gave you tough times. Pressures are meant to push forward and the opposite pressures play rival's or enemy's role to pull back for a fall or push hard, almost like throwing down, resulting the failure for onward move.

Imagine now your life, if there is no pressure, no worries, no target, no reason for work and all that needed are at your disposal, would you be thinking to be inspired, motivated and encouraged to do something and perform that kind of act which yields fruit, marks achievement and energizes you for further greater momentum?

Life without pressure is motionless, lifeless and dead. If at all possible, then let us hope and work for this kind of living, where we just need to stretch our hand, pluck the fruit from the tree, wrap it's leaves around us, cover ourselves and live under its shelter. What better or best man can be with such mind and mindset? What kind of world then this would be?

Sages and saints of all religious backgrounds who renounce and cut off their ties with the human society, wishes to settle down somewhere in the far hills, river banks or some secluded places. They no longer wish to be the partakers of the world that essentially moves ahead, moves well, moves with a meaning, for a meaning and moves forcibly under walloping pressures of life. They feel involved/lost in their new world without responsibilities for anyone/anything other than their meagre food, clothing and shelter.

All these comes to them without effort and work. The human society with millions and billions of duties and responsibilities that makes this world beautiful, powerful, meaningful, creative, innovative and existing with billions, trillions and googolplexes of things visible and invisible has a respectful, fearsome, honorable and soft corner for the world that clipped itself off from the responsible and duty-bound society.

It's a personal choice. There is equivalent respect for all kinds of people, sage's world or the other one, responsible or irresponsible, duty free or duty bound, careful or careless. Everyone though work, but does all that for themselves. We work collectively, but ultimately build our own worlds.

The issue arises when someone either tries, works, distracts, deviates or acts destructive against the common good. Human history sees such kinds of pro and anti-initiations every day and also the clash of the Titans for the same.

Bound to live under pressures and prove one's worth for one's own good or go against it and disprove oneself, is again a personal choice in conclusion. What we deal here is knowing pressure, understanding them, their positive and negative forces, facing them effectively, wisely, tactfully and successfully.

Our primary focus is handling pressures. Pressures are of different kinds; therefore, every pressure needs to be handled differently. We usually live under wrong impression that pressure is only against the weak, failing and the unsuccessful, but the fact is, the strong, succeeding and successful too had the same amount of pressure as of the former.

Let's go back to the genius and the just missed genius. The genius also was under the same pressure, hit from all corners of life, but was cool, patient, focused, wise and effective in handling it. Whereas the just missed genius got tensed, felt overpowered/overloaded, restless to beat the rival, impatient, jealous, wrongly focused at the competitor instead of the goal, unwise in handling.

Think of anyone who has no pressures, from infants to dying olds? We lay various kinds, but with a good intention to make them live well, work, be human and become something. Sometimes, we are wrong by placing beyond capacities, sometimes we are wrong by thinking overloaded and sometimes situations and circumstances drop unnecessary, unwanted and undeserving pressures.

Everything can be in control, only, if we change our view and thinking. It's just a thought and a decision that can change everything:

'I have a goal, I have a responsibility, it's my life, my duty, if not I, then who will make it? Nothing is too difficult, nor it is impossible. I can do all things and I can handle everything well.' Create positive energy sufficient to go against all pressures till we meet in next lesson.

Lesson 4
Killing Jealousy Or Killing Jealousy

Overcame from deep depression with the help of various counseling and therapies, the just missed genius fought back against all distracting and destroying powers. The battle wasn't easy, neither for the struggler, nor for the parents, counselors, teachers, advisers and therapists.

All was well but the expectations neither changed nor died in any of them. Now, the counselee is a recovered patient from mental imbalance, but none of them wish to put aside their expectations and ease the severity/intensity of the competition or the mark that got missed earlier.

Seeing at the recovery speed and rate, everyone thought that no more the same will be called just missed genius but the genius. It is good and right to be always in the race, but with thorough preparation, not under pressures, nor with any other intentions.

Everyone was seeing the bright side after recovery, hoping that miraculous and extraordinary powers might have taken birth because of expert's advices and help. Only the sufferer knows what the pain and agony is, what was lost and is at the verge to lose more.

Wanting to be at the top and regain all that lost glory, the aspiring genius doesn't wish to risk any more chances, but could not realize or come to know when jealousy again overpowered and constantly knocked until got distracted and deviated from the real path.

Days passed very fast and the curricular and extracurricular events were more than anyone interested to show the end of the academic year in the calendar. One after the other, the aspiring genius appeared in the tests and events. Apart from the curricular results, all other were instant at declaration.

The participation was mere attempt, but the performance was utterly flop and the results shattering.

Worried self, concerned parents, teachers and others went completely dumb and awaited curricular results. Curtains raised over the suspense, declaring the exam results, it's no more the just missed genius or aspiring genius but a very poor performer, who couldn't even race anywhere close to pass marks.

Now, the once depressed genius became an aggressive, arrogant and wild dummy. The scene totally changed opposite in direction and so far, beyond anyone's imaginations. The new aggressive individual turned a threat to all, especially to the genius. No more counseling, no more therapies, not even any advice worked, instead, the pressures, unknown and fears strange occupied everyone. Doctors, counselors and therapists were replaced by saints, sages, sorcerers, temples and shrines.

Leaving it a suspense for the remaining part and climax for now, moving ahead with certain observations and questions. Handling someone or self, post recovery either physical or mental needs proper understanding and guidance. Overloading with too much of sympathy or too much of sensitivity is both sickening further and deadly dangerous to recovery process.

Too little of care and too little of attention again is pathetically bad. Post recovery requires coping with the loss, considering it nothing and focusing ahead thinking, 'it's never late, not a big deal, nothing happened at all.' Doing this is not so easy as saying.

Not everyone has greater capacities and fighting spirits to cope up. Therefore, putting back the fighting spirit but in right amounts, in right direction and in right manner opens the graves for resurrection.

Was the aspiring genius too much focused, too much concerned, too sensitive, too delicate, so poor at handling pressures, making wrong steps in wrong directions or too competitive, too jealous, zero tolerant or too selfish?

Answers for all these can be here in the following sentence, but will that make way for generating pressure beaters in you? Surely, your answer is no.

Therefore, the final words for now will be, kill that jealousy before it kills you. Beat the pressure before it goes for a blast in you. How do you see this, 'killing jealousy' or 'killing jealousy'? Read that last sentence again till you get the difference, and thus, there lies all answers too.

Lesson 5
Born With You - Gone With You

I have no idea until someone told me, I haven't seen you even after many pointed out about you, I wasn't aware about your existence until scores of people accused me taking you along and playing spoil sport. It was impossible for me to accept that you were with me and hurt many people.

I questioned myself, am I blind or are you visible to all but invisible to me alone? Are you playing hide and seek with me? Are you my enemy, my back stabber, my spoiler, my destroyer? Who are you, how do you look, where have you pitched your tent inside of me? Why do you exist there? What do you do need of me? What do you want to do to me? What can I do that you leave me?

Aah! Come on tell me, it's enough now, I can't bear it anymore. Uhh, I never knew that you can be so mean, so selfish, so rude, so destructive until your presence was heavily felt and the damage was evidently visible, irreplaceable, Irrecoverable; pain, insult, shame and agony incurable and just worth lamentable. I wasn't aware yesterday, fully aware today but helpless for tomorrow because you grew so strong, mightier, overpowered and giant like feeding yourself on my feelings and actions.

Ashamed of yesterday, tensed of today and worried of tomorrow, I ask myself, 'is there a way to overcome, fight back overpower and blow the trumpet of triumph? Oh, my soul, all my senses, all my intelligence, all my strengths and powers, all my making and building constructive thoughts, I need to come out of this. Will you be my help, my support, my backing, my weapons, my armor, my soldiers, front foot warriors and obey my commands for battle and for triumph?

Where else can I look for help other than inside of me? Since, it's not the battle against outside enemies but against and with the ones inside of me, my own, who I unknowingly birthed, sheltered, nurtured, protected, prioritized, respected and employed for my envious means and missions.

Today, it refuses to detach from my inner being, vacate my mind, heart, soul and spirit. It goes ahead of me in everything needful and unnecessary, it never bows before my commands, nor is willing to be submissive to my orders. It has become my master, my commander and my lord.

Humiliated of myself for helpless me in its hands, guilty of carelessness, negligence and wrong ideas that made me no one, left me nowhere and of no worth.

Wise are they that recognizes its existence in the beginning and the wisest are they that plucks it out from the ground before it pitches its roots stronger and deeper inside, and spreads its branches wider, broader and in plenty occupying the whole being. I was a fool, uneducated about my own self, unaware about my being, my belongings, my friendly and envious inner self.

Taking the support of my wisdom and understanding, being trained in life lessons, grasping the knowledge of values and value systems, realizing and respecting the feelings of others, learning to love myself so I can love them as I love myself, teaching my heart not to covet what is not mine, explaining my mind that coveting is equivalent to stealing, robbing and forcefully looting, all that inside me is not my benefactors, well-wishers and truly working for me, I somehow convinced myself.

The process has just begun, baby steps are in progress, fall and rise slowly disappearing, strong moves are energized, perfectly determined, maturely anticipated for flawless walk and victorious conquest. Better late than never! Every thought from here, every step and move, every conflict and every success count for mastering myself.

Fighting against the battery of jealous armies, I stared at them and challengingly smiled, but the commander in chief, my enemy, who I birthed, nurtured and made strong responded to me in a one liner, 'born with you, gone with you, I'm jealousy, no one's friend but enemy of all'. Hearing this, I am strongly determined and equipped now to face it wisely, cleverly and tactfully.

Exercise gives confidence, confidence empowers next step, next step gives courage, courage gives success and success boosts confidence again cyclically. Do it, do now, Master Yourself.

Lesson 6
Just Miss - Total Miss

Slippers are meant to protect the sole from sharp, pointed, hurting, injuring dangerous objects. They are also intended to keep the feet hurt from hot and cold, muddy and dirty grounds. Shoes go beyond, giving more comfort, complete safety all around the feet up to the ankle. Workmen in heavy industries, hazardous surroundings, forests like areas need more safety, and so, the footwear designed for them are very special and specific.

Shoes and sandals also achieved the status symbol, became image builders and an inseparable part of well-groomed complete man. They look elegant, splendid and magnificent on man giving the same, unwavering confidence, flawless boldness and extra powerful shoulders to move into any kind, size, type of intellectual, philosophical, political, ideological or powerful individuals and crowds. But they go along with a condition, they must be own and well-fitting ones.

But sadly, painful and hurting, even in this internet age, there are millions of people who either cannot afford to buy sole protectors or the makers and the traders did not reach them yet. But still they move comfortably, confidently and with ease, because they have firstly adapted to such grounds and secondly their foot sole developed hurt and injury free self-protecting skin. They lay confidence not on rubber or leather protectors but on their naturally born skin. Most importantly among this crowd, many haven't either seen the footwear or never wore on them.

Therefore, it doesn't matter what they have on their shoulders or under their feet, but a clear vision and well-planned mission with undivided attention and keen focus on where to go, what to do, how to do, irrespective of the weathers, surfaces, surroundings, barriers, hurdles and challenges.

The poor, illiterate have no means to boost their morale, inspire to act, motivate to react and encourage to move ahead. They have no confidence boosters like eye appealing suiting and shirting, elegant accessories etc. If at all there is someone or something that fastens their belt to work tirelessly and restlessly in the assigned time frame of the day is the sunrise and sunset, of the longer periods is the change of climates.

There's no hesitation in saying that, apart from the above mentioned uses and benefits of footwear, there are many among the class and mass, literate and illiterate, educated and uneducated, well-mannered and ill mannered, cool and tempered kind of people, who use slippers, sandals and shoes for hurling at others.

One among such is our just missed genius, who entered the award ceremony event as an ill willing guest. When the rolls were called for honorary fields of excellence and the genius was one among the top, just missed genius very badly and poorly missed this list too. As a result, suffered fits like temper, volcanic temperature and nuclear blast in mind, felt almost the nerves in brain bursting.

The just missed genius was once well groomed, no compromise on apparels and accessories, appeared shabby today, walking away uncomfortably in someone else's unfitting shoes. All of a sudden and to everyone's shock the same removed both the shoes and swiftly threw one after the other at flashy speed towards the award receiving genius.

The celebratory atmosphere entirely turned tensed; the escorts ran in both directions immediately. The first group towards the genius for protection and the second group towards the just missed genius to arrest and handcuff. All that could be heard in the packed auditorium was of the screaming words of just missed genius, 'it's all because of you, you are the reason for my downfall, you are the culprit of my ruined life.'

How far was the just missed genius right as per the last statements? How valid are those accusations? Can blaming someone or accusing do any better to the already shattered life? Can someone really spoil others' lives? If so, what percentage/extent can the spoiler has the role to play? Does the just missed genius have any right to be jealous and destroy the genius?

Was the genius wrong by shining like twinkling star in all walks of life, that produces blazing jealousy in others and turns their everything and whole being into ashes? If you were the just missed genius, do you think you were right? If you were the genius, do you think it is wrong to be exceedingly excellent that causes envy and jealousy in others?

The bouncers escorted the genius to the podium, who is narrating success story. Whereas the just missed genius not just missed the podium and narrating success story but was insultingly carried away by the police to record the hateful happening's statement as investigation report. Be careful, just miss can become a total miss.

Lesson 7
Glory Mansion

Following the police jeep that rushed towards the local police station, worried, troubled, tensed, confused parents of just missed genius struggled to overcome the insult and made sure to free their ward by any means. Making calls to all influential and powerful people to be their help and recommend to the law keepers for mercy and compassion on them, they reached and gasped at the local police station.

Several hours passed, the parents were asked to remain outside in the lawn while the entire station continued on their works. Not everyone was swift in walk and talk, some were pathetically lethargic, some impatient, some short tempered, some harsh, some arrogant, some very rude.

Except for the higher ranks, all others appeared simply unconcerned of others' pains and situations. Midnight left its station, making way to the wee hours, while the sun was preparing itself to appear on the face of the earth, someone walked out and asked them to leave for now, since there is no way to free the ward at this point.

Unwillingly, with a heavy heart, the parents, friends and others gathered at the police station left to their respective homes. Few of the close, family and friends remained with them making calls and paying visits to their influential leaders.

Thankfully, the local leader agreed to be with them and marched to the station. Within minutes a large crowd gathered there comprising the leader's personal escort and the well-wishers of the just missed genius.

Requests turned into arguments and threats inside the station in charge cabin. Exchange of threats rained from both sides as the egos clashed very badly. Adamant upon the strictness, principles, rules and regulations, the inspector in charge made the stand clear and left the leader to bow before the required system of work.

Unable to do anything on own power and influence, the leader dialed to the superiors and more powerful leaders. All attempts failed before the uncorrupted inspector in charge, so the leader parted ways promising the parents to see them with help in the morning.

Motherhood of the just missed genius squeezed her heart, emboldened the guts, enlightened the understanding, empowered the vocals, enriched the reasoning and enforced her feet to move inside and appeal at least to see, if cannot free her child.

Seeing the tears, folded hands, but confident and well-reasoned appeals and statements of mother, the fatherhood in the inspector occupied the duty chair. Listened to all her child's, entire family's ordeal, and also realizing that the shabbily dressed one is none other than a genius, a just missed one, the inspector agreed to let the offender go upon her assurance to be there with her child in the morning.

Finding momentary and temporary relief, everyone reached home. The colleagues and subordinates in station looked pale at the strict, unbent inspector. Someone close dared to ask, what made you to go so concerned suddenly and soften your vocals dramatically?

The response was unexpected and unimaginable. He said, 'she fought against all her odds and projected that she hasn't given up yet in this battle to bring her child back to proper senses and make the just missed genius, the genius.'

Another heart wrenching response of the inspector that silenced the entire station dumb and squeezed everyone's hearts will be coming in the next lesson.

Ending here for you to ponder, what senses, emotions, feelings, intelligences and capacities you allow to work in you in tough, worst and crucial times?

A wrong thought, a wrong choice, a wrong decision always makes way for glory to depart and glory in turn makes way for shame and insult to march past and occupy the Glory Residence.

Lesson 8
Parting Glory - Marching Shame

Overcoming the outburst of emotions that are ready any moment to weaken him again, the inspector in charge adjusted his vocals to break the deafening silence that has overshadowed the entire atmosphere. Every ear attentive and every breath held indefinitely for what was going to be said. A moment later he began to narrate his traumatic side.

'Few years ago, joy, happiness, energy, enthusiasm, glory, honor, pride and life departed my house giving way to sadness, grief, apathy, dishonor, insult, shame, hopelessness and lifelessness. All my dreams shattered, just like the mansions built on weak foundations collapse at the hit of a strong wind and gushed waters.

All I could see was everything under the shambles. I looked for hope here and there, it's nowhere seen. I left my place to search for it. All that stood was something blurry in front of my sight, but it was too far to clear the vision.

I moved little further, but all alone. None of my people could make moves to go further and see whether that perfect one in my blurry vision is hope or not.

When I began to walk in search of hope, my family was with me. A little later they said, it might be blurred appearance to you, but for us is complete blind. We cannot walk further with you. My family failed to see hope and gave up resisting against the rolls called of those ready to mark themselves absent in the rolls of the living.

Once, my wife was in the same position as of this woman today. She too pleaded me with folded hands and moist eyes to have mercy upon her child. My child too was in the same position and situation as of this woman's. I was asked to be soft, compassionate, reasonable, understanding, adjusting, tolerant and patient.

But none of those pleadings, suggestions, advices and even criticisms worked on me. I was adamant on my stand, my vision, my goal, my way of living, working, thinking and my harsh, vigorous disciplined method of becoming not just something or someone but the great so and so.

I was mercilessly imposing my schedule, my methodologies and my style of making oneself on my child. There would be no single day where I would be leaving to my work without tons and loads of harsh Imposing, and would be taking the account of the same from my child after returning from my duties.

I used to assign the duty of task master to my wife to see the child obeys and follows all my instructions with anticipated results, failing which I would turn beast on both. You must never be someone or something but the great, the best, the genius etc. was my uncompromised warning.

Every time I wished that my child must be the topper, the genius and the great, but I was disappointed by the same with either just missed genius or badly missed genius. Pressures increased very badly from my side. I never could understand that each one has own capacities and capabilities.

As a result, my child dropped gradually in the numbers and grades and finally plunged to the utterly missed genius from just missed genius. But still, neither was there any change in my attitude nor my way of thinking. No compromise was my strong words to my child as a daily reminder.

It is good to set goals, give targets, hard exercises, additional explorations and also to strictly make our wards understand the need, necessity and importance to be on the top ranks, but I failed to understand that pressure mounting is entirely different from the foresaid. Unable to take the loads dumped, my child lost the mental balance and was shifted to trauma center. It's been years, my child is just alive but living dead.

My child first failed to see the hope, because I and my imposing stood tall and huge like mountains between them. Next, my wife too could not see hope at all, because my shadow around her was so shady and dark that she went blind in its scary effect. Unable to bear my animosity she decided to go absent from this, especially my horrific, traumatic and terrible world. My child though living, but is almost absent like the mother.

It took complete loss but understanding was adamant and was unwilling to meet me and be with me. Thankfully and finally, understanding gave up and made hesitant moves towards me but not before another genius missed the mark and another mother pleaded same words before me. It is up to me now, how well and how long I can keep understanding with me and move along wisely, rightly and flawlessly.

Lesson 9
Mad Expectations

Lost in my world, buried under the flood of shame and insult, the inspector in charge started a new battle, unknown and strange to him. He is illiterate, unarmed, untaught and inefficient in this new warfare. His ego, pride, arrogance and superior attitude chained him and plastered his lips from asking help. All through his life he chose to remain unhelped, uncomforted, unsympathised lone warrior. This attitude imprinted the idea as patented thought it him.

Therefore, he expects everyone to be self-learned, self-dependent, self-sufficient and self-motivated soldier, student, professional and success oriented individual. He hates the lazy and lethargic, he hates to see people leaning on others and supports, he hates spoon feeding, he gets fumed at the failing and struggling individuals.

He is mad at compromises, merciless at cheating and bribing, he is cruel at disobedient and undisciplined. Hence, the new battle was fighting shame and insult, and to live in the glory departed suffocating shameful mansion. The new feelings he had to face and undergo were alien lesser, but piercing pins and thorns more. He feels like sitting and lying on those thorny chairs and cots. The air was contaminated with hate that developed against the failing and failed lives of his spouse and child.

It was because of the resultant life they left behind against his wishes and expectations. He didn't forget them even after their lives got disastrously ruined, who actually was supposed to be apologetic, but there was no remorse at all on his face. He didn't stop to accuse and accurse them for mishandling their lives. He has a strong belief and principle that iron must sharpen and cut the iron. So, he justified his harsh stand against them. It wasn't that he had no feelings, no love, no concern for them, but his strictness, discipline, rules and regulations have overpowered them. Adding more spice to his system, he chose his profession accordingly. The position and rank he holds poured in extra fuel to authoritative and commanding mindset. Beyond all these, he never allowed anyone to find heart routes and be his adviser, counselor, friend and even a well-wisher.

Can anyone dare cross his lines? Can there be any hope for such, the so called great? Who can rope into his nostrils and mend him? Why are the heavens and the gods so blind and mute unto his actions? Why so much power is given to one man in the family? How can he alone take such powerful stance and leave everyone else in the family voiceless, choiceless, freedom-less and powerless? Why and how can he alone have all the life and the rest lifeless? How unfair it is that he holds the sole decision-making authority and the others just puppets?

Why did everyone allow him to have even their share of boldness, guts, authority and let him take the face of terrifying and threatening upper hand? Why all his parents, elders, siblings, families failed to notice and clip off his fangs like venomous character right at the tender stages? Who all shall I blame, were his wife's endless questions concluding with etcetera, etcetera, etcetera at the end page of her dairy before ending her life abruptly? The question followed these were, the situations in my life didn't yet reach the budding stage. Will there be any hope that I can see it blossom?

Your answers, reasoning in the case can give you plenty of lessons, very particularly life lessons. You surely are fitting into one of the characters, the genius, just missed genius, the mother with folded hands, the inspector in charge, poorly missed genius or the mother with endless questions?

Lesson 10
Poisonous Pen - Wide Opened Eyes

How many times should I remind you to wake me up with bed coffee? Switch on the television and get me the newspaper. Put on the geyser, come on, I am getting late. Did you keep my uniform ready? How about shoes, are they polished? My shoes are not shining, they should reflect my image on them. Take them back and polish again. Uniform too is not properly ironed, do it again. Is my lunch ready? Where is my hand kerchief? I don't find my watch; did you see my keys?

Tonight, guests will be there with me for dinner. One is a pure vegetarian, another loves sea food, make sure there is both fish and prawns of different varieties. A friend of mine is allergic to spices and the other is lover of the same. See that they shall be served accordingly. Be careful while you serve tea and coffee. Two likes tea but one takes green. Another is lover of coffee, so serve in large mug. The other takes coffee but without sugar. Bear this in mind while you serve desert too.

Why is the pet barking, leave everything aside and take it out first? Leaves are turning yellow, aren't you watering plants well? Did you make my bed? Why didn't you change the bed sheets and pillow covers? Switch on the mosquito repellent and put off the lights. I want music, soft. Play in low volume.

All these are daily rants. Pat comes the reply for every sound and the work too gets done promptly along. But today, only one-sided sound, no response from the other side. These questions and commands echoed back from the silenced walls. No one to hear, no one to respond, no one to work. 'How many times I have to tell you to come with my bed coffee?' The silence and no response from here continued till the last one, 'I want music, not soft, but sad.'

He got so tired doing all extra chores, his personal, which usually gets done by spouse and child. He was still adamant to accept and express the grief, pain and loss of his family. He grew stubborn, who doesn't wish to give scope for any sympathetic feelings to take birth. He was even maintaining that nothing was wrong on his part, strongly blaming them for not being able to withstand against the pressures.

Several days, weeks and months passed with this daily chanting routine but couldn't realize how heavily he loaded their backs. He does nothing except getting ready, eating and drinking his share and retiring to bed after returning back from work.

The house looks very dirty, dust and cobwebs all over, dirty bed and sofa linen, curtains and others. His wife's and child's wardrobe were untouched since that day. Being a self-disciplined person, it was impossible for him to live without personal and his house maintenance. So, today he wished to clean the entire house and started one after the other.

He reached her wardrobe and almost spent the entire day there. He didn't move from that place, not because he was emptying it, cleaning and setting it back. But because his eyes were scanning through the pages that had so much of venom and hurt.

All that venom was consumed, not a single drop was left by her. But neither that venom nor its power can get ever except when its writer chooses to strike them off, tear those pages or forgives the one that is the reason for hurt and poisonous life.

The pen that ran over the paper with venomous ink was part of his wife's diary. He could not believe his eyes that she had so hard feelings against him and could even write so bad about him.

All the above rants too appeared in her diary, but he feels it is his right to get the things done. What's wrong in that? But his wife has complaint not against the works she was made to do, but the hardened heart and merciless behavior.

Facing the just missed genius' mother, realization began to work in him, but after reading the astonishing lines, the real man in him began to awake. Her hitting lines were, 'how can you be so mean, stubborn, thoughtless and cruel against making your stand always right? You can never feel that there's someone or somebody else also living, not you alone.

I wish that, at least these words may awaken real man in you, after I leave this world. But still, you can't be good to anyone. I can only hope that you realize how wrong you were, before you too write your last page and last line on this earth and then vanish. Please don't leave any traces of your remembrances. They hurt so bad, they hurt to death.'

Lesson 11
Writing On The Wall – Venomous Ink

Pressing on the pause button at the reflecting dairy reading for a while, let us spend some time at analyzing and drawing conclusions of who was right and who wasn't. We have seen both the inspector in charge and his wife and also their child.

Leaving the child aside, since we have dealt with almost similar life of the just missed genius in detail, let us move ahead with the parents. To make you understand, we will be seeing at another case called a suicidal but not deliberate accident.

While you were pressing the untrained accelerators and brakes, steering undertraining wheels, looking through the inexperienced rearview mirrors and windshield, switching the tensed signal buttons on and off, all with an L-Board, the people in front, back and besides alert themselves, because you have given them a very clear and loud signal to keep themselves safe.

The purpose of the learning board is to make everyone in the vicinities aware that you are not a learned driver. Therefore, any accident, God forbid, if at all takes place, you will be having a forgivable safe corner, unless it is not deliberate. And the victim is to be blamed for not being cautious and attentive to escape that untoward mishap.

This is very similar to hanging 'beware of the dog.' If you trespass into their premises, despite the board has warned you, you will not just be liable to treat your own injuries, if at all the animal attacks you but also for prosecution.

The driver whether learned or unlearned, by any chance runs the vehicle into accident, except for the insurance claim purposes and legal proceedings, in case the damage is big and injures are bad, it won't attract any investigative procedures. In case, if someone/others are hurt, their properties or vehicles get damaged, then you will be liable for legal prosecution. Beyond that, not only you will be asked to bear the damages but also the medical bills.

Life lessons too, if they are with baby steps and inexperienced, uncontrollable accidental wrongs, they will be having the grace of forgivable soft nature. But repeated and deliberate ill mannered, undisciplined, disrespectful, stubborn, arrogant, rigid, adamant, unlawful, unwarranted, harsh, cruel, beastly, demonic characteristics and respective behavior, attitude, nature and character usually possess unpardonable, unmerciful and unconditional befitting response. But this differs from person to person.

What we have said is the common reaction at large. Right from the beginning, we have maintained our stand leaning on to the diffuser's side. This entire course is to install or have diffusers. Those with diffusers can pardon, ignore, let go off any grave hurt, damage and loss too. Even they go to the extent of settling any dispute or loss that has entered judicial premises too.

The inspector was a learned, well-trained expert at life lessons. He is highly matured, both at age and experience. His learnings and practices of self-reliance are exceptionally commendable. They are worth honored, awarded and quoted as best exemplary. His will to withstand any worst circumstance and overcome all lacks of life is highly appreciable. The way he defeated and left behind all odds, including utter poverty and hopelessness, qualifies to be life lessons for the strugglers and the poor with high ambitions.

'But', this single word separates his life totally different from what is said so far. If at all anyone's life stands several great qualities and attributes commendable, then that sentence must never have the factual and contrary word that is also an exposer of the other side of reality, but his strict nature unknowingly developed very strong, sharp, piercing, fierce, fearsome, cruel, beastly and sometimes demonic reactors too.

Every time he reacts strongly against any action, he directly charges, recharges, feeds, nurtures, empowers and loosens the string of control over his ready to attack powers. He could have ignored some, pardoned some, gave a deaf hearing to some, compassionate smile to some and could have avoided some. Since his nature of duty demands every minute detail very important, crucial and not to be missed at any chance, he failed to keep that demand, kind of dealing away from personal and family life. His social life too has not many colors, it is simply pale or black and white.

How would you see yourself at this juncture? How different are you from this character or how similar/closely you resemble to the same? If your accident is deliberate, or you are a thoroughly trained poor driver, then won't you be liable for prosecution? If you make wrong choices that only affects you and no one else, then your suicidal accident, learned but poorly managed life leaves you nowhere.

Accelerate not because the road is smooth, worth racing, but according to need and your control capacity. Apply brakes well, only if needed, avoid accidents and let the journey proceed. Control the steer, keep it from any distractions, deviations and wrong diversions. Have well trained drive, safe and joy wheels all the time!

Lesson 12
Reflections – Introspecting Mirror

Releasing the pause button to continue what the inspector's shocked scanning eyes with speechless mouth too widely opened on the teary pages of his totally diffused wife, because of the explosive nuclear power of her husband's reactive nature, we found that both of them got powers divided unfairly. One is with too much of explosions and the other with too much of diffusers.

'I never uttered a single word against you, since it might hurt you and either make you mad or put you completely down. I wasn't worried about your madness, but was very scared that you cannot take it rightly and might lose mental balance and slip into coma. I know how much you respect your image and cannot allow anyone to cross your lines.

You have painted yourself a 'perfect living soul' image. You think that you will never make mistakes and never give chance to anyone ever say that you were wrong in such and such way. It is good and I am very proud of your flawless type of dealing and living, but not until I lost my child for your over discipline, extra strictness, too much involvement and constant warnings.

Your love and concern are so big, even bigger than mine, but it never came out with right emotions, feelings and appropriate expressions. They have always felt pierced, because in your everything you put forward your judgmental mindset.

All our enjoyment would instantly get buried in between the deep layers of your strict restrictions. They seem to vanish just like the evening sunlight upon the entry of darkness. All that happiness and celebrations with high spirits, where every last energy drop of good feelings are released to fill the soul and spirit, shaking legs, matching vibes with others, tuning everyone into one tone, one tempo and one style, turns sadly, unwillingly and painfully attracting attention like posture before the commanding chief.

I was silent, am silent and will be silent till I count my last breath and release it forever. These lines are between you and me. No one knows, and you too let it not be found by anyone. I know you are into pieces after reading them, but a surgeon's scissors, knives, needles and threads are meant to give life, nothing else. The process is removing killing deadly pain by giving little pain through surgeries, injections etc. Consider my lines for the same and read this till the last pages.

I used to keep this in your reach to let you know what, how, my child and I feel, but you never bothered to touch it. I respect you for this alone, since, at least you have respected my privacy. But I didn't wish that. Everything happened and mostly you did everything contrary to my wishes.

I don't know how you would react after reading this, but reading this after I am no more there with you will add no meaning. So, I don't care for your reaction, because I had seen numerous outbursts so far. Another or some more or a nonstop rain of mad outbursts from here, I don't fear them anymore, but I wish you find this and read.'

The inspector did not dare to go to another page and therefore paused reading. The last lines were common on every page, wanting to sound stern warning. But sadly, the warning bells did not reach his ears as she wished.

In the past we used to see the vehicles, especially busses, trucks, tractors etc. heavily loaded and leaning to one side, as if they might tumble down anytime. As per the load shifted, it appears they are being pulled up to sides rather than moving straight and smooth. Many such vehicles have broken down on the main roads, spilling all that carrying loads, sometimes good for nothing, like milk, oils, grains etc.

A bad vehicle is not so greatly responsible as that of a bad loading, except for the greed of the bad vehicle's owner. Sometimes the hesitation and incapability to say no of the same too leads to bad loading. The loss in anyways is on both sides.

Inspector's wife would have resisted the reactors in a right way, which actually she knows. She could have let him known slowly and little by little. She could have overcome the sulking silence and made sound reasoning. She could have taken the advantage of liberty at any moment and discussed, saying, there is another better way always for everything. She failed to opt for the other better way than silence and so failed to present an option before her husband for the alternative choices.

She was right in respecting her husband's feelings, but was wrong when right things were expected in wrong ways and wrong things in wrong ways. Having diffuser doesn't mean going silent and mute. It doesn't even mean you don't resist by placing your view point. It is neither leaving everything to bear unnecessary pains nor allow our backs for loads that we cannot carry.

Leaving it here for introspection, since life is attached with so many people around, it is not a single journey. Though, you are all alone, may be a bachelor, spinster, divorced, orphan etc., but your life is associated and tied to so many strings that you come across, deal with and relate to in your daily life.

You can avoid discussions or arguments that have least prominence, unnecessary debates that have no gain but only loss, meaningless quarrels with quarrelsome people, since such natures cannot be changed. But you can very well deal with people associated in the close-knit family wisely, tactfully, cleverly, lovingly, respectfully and by taking chances and even risks.

Mastering Myself is not simply controlling anger, short temper etc., but mastering winning ways that blows triumphant trumpet at every relation, every dealing by winning yourself first with all right moves and reactions.

Lesson 13
Life Cards – Bad Players

Giving end - taking end; sending end - receiving end; making end - breaking end, the list is endless at every point, situation, speech and deal. Out of both the ends, there are people who have plenty and they give accordingly, there are people who have little, so they give little, there are others who have very little and they give likewise and there are some others who have nothing to give but are in position only to take.

This applies for any and every case. You give according to the amount and capacity you possess. It could be some generous gifts, some charity, some alms; it could be great respect, honor, happiness, laughter, energy, strength, support, confidence, and blessings etc.

If you stand at the receiving end and the giving end has too little or nothing to give, then you will be a poor man having so little treasures that fundamentally and only comes from the outer sources. It is good to give sparingly, bountifully, if that item, amount, thought or idea makes someone's day and life. It is better to give a supporting hand and it is best to make an uplifting favor by enlightening, educating and empowering.

Imagine yourself among the poor, very poor, broken and insolvents and you happen to be at the receiving end all the time, what good they have to give you? Expecting from the insolvent, broken and very poor, you feel dead with shame and guilt.

But you have no option other than to give what you have. There are things that can be refilled, reproduced and recreated just like a battery on a running vehicle, having no additional charger but gets recharged on the run. It usually doesn't drain of its charge other than left idle without use.

Energies, good wishes, good feelings, good humor, good thoughts etc. have recharging capacities, even if it is one sided. But sadly, there is something called expectation, which plays bad role every now and then, and destroys all foundations of selflessness.

Imagine now that you are living among the rich and the ultra-rich, who has so much to give and can only give. They are rich and are generous in giving but very poor in receiving. All that they have, they usually don't give but pour and dump on others. All their bad temper, tantrums, frustration, irritation, hate, enmity, strife, jealousy, blame and every other kind of poison. How burdened, broken, troubled, tensed, helpless and hopeless you look!

Living among the poor in every good thing and living among the bountiful in every bad thing is a reduced state of life, that has no hope for anything better. If others cannot be of any help, then it is neither an issue nor a loss of anything. But, if someone takes away, snatches, or destroys what we have, created and built, then it is certainly a great loss.

It brings along angry, hurt, hatred and revengeful feelings against the destroyer of peace, possessions and all the developed stages and areas of life. This can even go to an extent of never rising back to the lost glory and might completely put away the fighting spirit.

This is what we have seen in the lives of the just missed genius, the inspector and his wife. Each one is very rich and very poor in many things. So, their lives took miserable turns, where no one is in a position to return back to their balanced senses.

One has put an abrupt dead end for any sense to function, the other lost almost all the senses except jealousy, hatred and grudge. The third is so strong, so perfect, so powerful, so rich in everything but very poor in measuring the same.

He doesn't know which ingredient weighs more and which less and which one very little to make a delicious, aromatic and nutritious dish. He failed to understand that life though has VIBGYOR colors, but can give million shades upon right mixing.

None of the three played a winning role and neither anyone stood supportive and constructive. They were all very bad players of life cards; they were very poor in both giving and receiving the right things.

They even were very bad in ignoring, neglecting and letting go off what was unimportant, unnecessary, harmful, troublesome and destructive. None of them were at the winning side but breaking side. Everyone broke others' hearts.

Lesson 14
Not In My Backyard

No doubt, I love you so much, I admire you, respect you. You are more than my life, my interests, my happiness, my world, my everything. You stand before everyone, you hold the highest regard, you are always there in my mind, thoughts. You have occupied my entire space. Every single cell of my body, if split into individuals, then each one will contain only you. My mind had never thought anything keeping you aside, nor can I ever imagine doing so.

You are inseparable. Separating myself from you can be called anything like suicide, euthanasia, strangulation, slow poison etc. In sharing and caring, extra portion, including the sacrificial never ever fell on my side.

Racing towards the victory stands, when you and I had to beat one another, I go limping, hurt and with all dramas to push you ahead. Standing on the same platform and sing, I don't know from where but sore throat advances its way to see you on the presentation platform. You name it, anything and everything registers your name. I don't know till today why, but I am not I, I am you. I'm nothing without you.

I never cared what the world might say to this, in fact, I had come across many inexpressible remarks, criticisms, comments and gossips, but gave a deaf ear, blind eye, absent myself. They scratched their heads, pulled their hairs, bit their nails, tore their robes, gone crazy and nuts on failing to give this bond a name, a relation.

Their madness at our bond could have been a reason for easy outburst, but it always went against everyone's expectations, and for me it wasn't less than any amusement. Seeing our thrilling adventurous closeness in every walk and talk, the world has burnt extra calories unnecessarily.

They could not notice when time ran away from their precious to do lists, money fell short to jump into their pockets and banks, blood in their nerves raced faster than usual for no reason, and minds got struck like densely populated city street traffic jams. Looking at all these, every time my pride would climb onto the Everest peaks, hoist the jealous flag for others, and would enjoy till the last feel of that great emotion gets exhausted.

My expressions in all these used to be celebratory, luminous with the touch of dangerous voltage and blasting thunderous sound with high decibel wattage. A story, a biopic, a short film cannot do much justice to our relationship, unbroken bond, selfless and highly respected, not two but one in mind, soul and body. Anything lesser than a feature film or a novel will be an insult by undermining, understating and underrating our characters.

I never resisted you even when your affectionate portions made ways unto me. But, one thing with sternness in my unwavering vocals, I politely say, 'not in my backyard.' Yes, If I sound soft, low, apologetic, hesitant and feared here, I would be destroying all that I said so far. If I silently allow you to dump all the trash, which actually is not yours, and myself your dumping land, then you will make it a practice, a habit, a routine, an act unresisted and would fill yourself with all mad trash and keep dumping over me.

There is room for command, authority, greater than request, demand to fulfill all your rightful wishes, desires, feelings and needs but no compromise, zero tolerance for unrightful madness that you create thinking you have a kick bag to punch, kick and release your pressures, frustration, irritation and anger.

I cannot allow myself to be a blind and mute receiver of whatever you dump on me. You will always have a shoulder to lean and cry whenever any unfortunate, untoward, hurting, sad, failing and tragic accidental, natural, unnatural calamities or caused by some known and unknown reasons but not any part of me for your unnecessary outbursts.

My resistance can be your madness initially, even after sometime and forever, but you must understand that you have every right to make anyone feel good and happy, but not for a sorry state and sadness. You can give all that you have, but I have a choice whether to accept, receive or take them.

You will be my head, my crown, my glory as long as you have winning attitude. No one can bring you down from there other than breaking ways and hurting nature. Resist, respect. Try somewhere else, but not in my backyard. Do this, you will find differences and values.

Lesson 15
Trailing Winners – Winning Breakers

It is an age-old question, accompanied by many more, why do the wicked flourish? Why does the bad people have big share in all the good things? Why does the wrong doers succeed in all that they do to trouble, disturb, destroy and demolish all the good schemes of humble and right people? Why on earth that the evil power appears mightier than the upright?

Why do the heavens remain silent, if at all everything is clearly visible? Why doesn't someone come to the rescue when the destructive, abusive and demonic forces work through the rascals of the society? Why do the laws and systems appear weak before the so-called strong offenders, criminals, thieves, dacoits, looters, cheats and fugitives? Why was I born in the midst of such surroundings that has no respect for others?

Is there any world that is free from all wrong practices, injustices, inequalities, selfishness and mean mentalities? Is there any hope for the humble, soft, kind and tender hearted to rule this world? If so, when can this gentle portion of humankind be fortunate to such blessed state of living? What could be such great contribution that would make the cool, calm and minding own business generations pour in their efforts to see the heavens built on earth?

If heavens are real then why are they so distantly far from man seeing them, entering and experiencing them? If heavens really are the dreamy worlds that have no presence of what mankind suffers badly here, why did this mortal race fail to reach immortal stage?

Finally, gasping and breathing hard, ending the infinite list of what I wanted but did not get, what I didn't want but got, what I resisted but was forced to have and live with the same, etc., leaving up to you to either answer, act, contribute, initiate, inspire, ignite, revolutionize or just read and fill mind sipping hot tea and do nothing.

Wanted to make someone's day special, great and memorable, wishing Happy Birthday with a delicious, attractive and appealing cake, promising a candle light dinner and with many other surprises, the day began well.

But suddenly, something wrong happened by that special person of the day, and as a result, fierce exchange of hot nouns, verbs, adjectives and adverbs rushed and got heaped on both sides. The lovely, happy, special and remarkable day indeed turned very great and eternally memorable, but contaminating the air with so much of anger, poison and hate.

What good it is to get engaged with such people who cannot resist few hours to let that special day specially pass, and what better it is again to that special person of the day, who cannot let off all those disturbances that would spoil memorable days? Resisting and controlling as said above must not limit only for the special days but for all days to make every day a special one.

The inspector's wife was poor at resistance, good at making herself a dumping yard. She appeared as if with a sign board, 'you can dump here'. Many people do have such nature. Their resistance power is very weak, their carrying capacities look extremely great, but really don't know what to do when the trash runs over them and bury underneath. They have little reasoning and logical senses to put things equally on the balance.

The character in the previous session was stern resistant type and the one just mentioned is no nonsense type. All three types are strong in their way of dealing, but the outcome purely depends on the other side. What we see here and learn is not just making oneself strong and right in actions and reactions, but also polishing, shaping and transforming the others too.

The first kind of character was senselessly silent, the second was sensibly vocal and the third was foolishly loud. Hence, it should be the attitude, daily effort, life's practice of every individual to keep, make and create each one's days splendidly marvelous and eternally historic.

Concluding here, the trailing winners and the winning breakers, which means, the people with winning others' hearts always seem trailing or falling short whereas the ones who are habitual heart breakers keep winning.

A step, a move is the beginning of the journey. So, contribute yours for this revolutionary journey. In the next lesson we will be seeing how in other ways, the so-called strong powers be overpowered by making ourselves really strong.

Lesson 16

Strong Powers - My Assets, My Liabilities

We call them forces, powers, energies, life agents, our friendly natural resources. We are nothing without them, in fact lifeless. The shortage and complete scarcity of such makes life burdensome and miserable. Some admire them, some enjoy them differently than usual usage, consumption, experiencing, some even worship them. Their enormous strength, power, force, ability etc. made man to move ahead beyond admiration and adoration.

We consider it nature evolved or created creation. We live in it, we love it, we enjoy it, we go around to see its beauty and marvel. What we did not make or create, but is far-far ahead and greater in all strengths and powers is always a threat. We see water, air, fire, sun and earth as the essential elements of life.

They are indeed. Each one has a different and unique purpose. None of them are similar in nature and works. Though the sun and fire have hot qualities, but both doesn't work in same manner. Similarly, the winds and waters have cooling nature, but life turns dead when we are left with alone with either of them.

For the survival of man, animals and birds, both are essentially needed life agents, not anyone. Call it the beauty of the nature, if you are an atheist or call it the beauty of creation, if you are a theist, irrespective of man's beliefs, it releases each and every force, power, energy in needful limited or prescribed amounts.

Sometimes, when we see it releasing the same in excess quantities, there occurs damages great, sometimes measurable, sometimes immeasurable, sometimes recoverable, sometimes irrecoverable. But this act and the damage/loss caused to properties, goods, fields, beast, foul and human life is called a natural act, natural calamity.

Whether it is due to excess of winds, rains, shaking of earth, fire in the forest, drought in the summer, nothing is called deliberate, accidental, vengeful of grudge, and none of them attracts any action against such acts. Hence, they look like the strong powers and forces, our life agents at the same time for some or no reason they can be our life snatchers too.

We have been seeing the emotions, feelings and expressions of man's life's happenings, resulting in actions and reactions as his strong powers, friendly assets and friendly liabilities too. Unlike the nature's excess, extra powerful actions, none of man's outbursts or hurting actions and reactions can be called natural damage or disaster, but an offense, deliberate and intentional. Such deeds naturally attract fitting responses or vengeful reactions.

Seen in the previous lessons and also above, that anything in limited or prescribed format is our asset and out of it, either excess or less is our liability. Having known and understood very clearly about our strengths, we must be careful and mindful so as to not let them become our liability anytime and at any cost.

Moving back to where we left the inspector going through the diary penned not with ink but with poison, the one which he had ignorantly produced in his wife's heart. If you believe that your good wishes, smiles and kind gestures have miraculous powers, then you must even admit that your bad words, unkind behavior, hurting nature too has disastrous powers.

All that you do outside of you, but in front of, to, with or for others has direct and indirect relation with them. Therefore, your everything, that moves out of you finds a store, dwelling or room in others.

What all the inspector did, got stored in his wife and child. Similarly, what all his wife and child did or didn't do got stored in him. The mother and the child were hurt and therefore were looking for a transformation in him. Inspector too felt like the child was spending the interest, focus and concentration part somewhere and so was missing the mark, also his wife failed to help the child reach there, for which he was expecting improvement in both.

Whatever it may be, but all three of them failed to open their stores for appropriate measures of life's dealing agents, their strong powers. Being ignorant, being negligent, being careless, being reckless amounts to one and the same, bad results.

Rise from where you have fallen, start from where you got stopped, learn from where you have failed, gain from where you have lost, turn from where you got diverted, concentrate from where you got distracted, focus from where you got deviated, correct from where you have gone wrong and have hope from where you went hopeless.

This is what the inspector sighed after going through all the pain filled pages of his departed wife's poisonous diary. Recollecting an immortal bird, Phoenix associated with the Greek mythology, that cyclically regenerates or is otherwise born again, the inspector began a new but very different chapter in his life.

Call it a transformation, eye opening or regeneration like phoenix, which is believed to move close to sun, gets burnt into ashes and from there arises again of its predecessor.

Whatever it may be, let us assume the scorching heat from his wife's diary, or the irrecoverable partial loss, one dead, the other living dead.

He has challenged himself to bring back just the missed genius and his own child utterly missed genius back to life normal. He has his spirit risen back to the previous state, but in more than powerful and in right ways. And so, he headed to breathe life in both the geniuses and make them prove that missed mark or target is temporary not permanent. Except for the life lost physically, no life departed from other areas of living is eternal.

Lesson 17
Chipping Off Extra Rock

A dynamite is not the idea and tool of a sculptor, neither he ever brings the thought of having such explosives into use for his carvings, rather, a chisel and a hammer appears to be his friendly inseparable tools. Whenever he sees a rock, he sees a picture, an image, a beautiful thing, person or animal stuck with extra pieces of rocks all around.

So, he never carves any image but chips off the extra rock, grinds the remains of the same, cleanses the dust remains in this whole process and then begins to adorn it, so that the buyers are pleased, got lost in its beauty, wanting to participate in the auction and keep voicing their say until each one feels I can't afford to buy it anymore.

The inspector too felt like chipping of his extra, unnecessary, harsh, over disciplined nature that got accumulated on his child in a wrong way and left the same for nothing but a traumatized individual. He didn't wait even a minute but rushed to the rehabilitation center to see his child whom he loved so much but was very poor at expressing, in fact, totally failed to express.

His steps rushed swiftly, got into the vehicle, his foot refused to step on to the brake pedal, but only got stubborn and pressurized to press on the accelerator. Ignoring the traffic, the system and even putting all other senses on absent mode and hurried on the way. The foot that was unwilling so far hit the brake pedal with all force at once, bringing the speed to dead zero.

Hurriedly he ran to the reception, impatiently waited to get the permission, hastily ran after getting the nod. But all this abruptly climaxed once he reached his child's room. His feet now refused to step ahead, they have chained and glued themselves to the floor, since his heart got filled with grief, agony, guilt and sorrow state. All his bodies respected the inner feelings and stood still like immovable statutes.

Looking at the beauty of the unity of all the bodies who honors, silences themselves and accompanies the grief stricken, sad, failure and broken upon something, but taking the advance position, the best place and celebratory upon something good, great and marvelous happening, the entire staff too involved themselves in the former mood accompanying all his bodies, they too stood still unmoved.

Standing at the entrance and looked through the glass, his child is with the therapists and counselors, so unwillingly controlled himself so as to not disturb them. But the eagerness inside did not allow him to be so courteous and respectful. And hence, he tuned the door knob and pushed the door gently.

His child looked at the father who appeared in a very different posture, which never ever saw even upon very close one's death, including his wife. The child has several question marks on the face, where as the father first time appeared without any commands, questions, orders, sounds, powerful actions and expressions including the answer to none of the child's silent, unsaid but facial questions.

Standing still there at the door, looking pale at his child without either blinking his eyes or moving any other part of his body, the father tried to judge all the emotions that went on protest like situation, but putting the grief and repentance in front, he finally allowed sorrow to take the stage and go ahead with the next act.

Getting the nod from its master, a drop of tear representing the whole act somehow found place to enter in his eyes. But the passage was not clear to slip down from there, because the father held it tight trying to push it back. But all the bodies together increased their support and squeezed his heart by pressing on the rewind and play button.

The little drop got some more moisture added to it and succeed to move a bit further with the push of all emotions. Sliding a bit further, still standing at the edge of the eyeball, is about to get dried if more support is not sent. Reading the tear's signal well, all the emotions at once made the father look at the child with sorry feeling.

Finally, that first drop of tears won the fight and slid suddenly down on to his cheeks. Following this one after the other, the tears gushed out and swiftly rolled down through his cheeks. He could not stop his emotions anymore, and cried out loud, screaming, 'I am sorry! I'm sorry my child!'

Seeing this strange change and the emotional outburst, the utterly missed genius got loaded with another ton of questions. Leaving the frozen state, the father moved close to his child and wept bitterly, all the while saying, I am sorry.

Lesson 18
Right Expressions

Genuine love, true compassion, heartfelt sympathy, unconditional care, what can replace them or work quicker, faster, and more effectively in healing emotional hurts? What best can replace 'I am sorry', that has immeasurable power to strike off and erase years and decades old misunderstandings, grudges, stubborn enmities?

Having come to know these mighty wonder working powers, the father began to be the best medicine, most effective cure and the natural healer of his child. The kind of diagnosis, cure and medicine in case of our own, who suffered due to our mistakes, deliberates, ignorant but wrongs are not found in any medical learnings and teaching books other than human understanding and the expression of the same.

So, with tears flowing from his eyes like streams of water passing through various turns, ups and downs, he didn't bother them but went and laid his hand first on the shoulder, after an uncontrollable few seconds hugged tightly and began to kiss and feel sorry. Here, he entered into the shoes of natural healer and the sculptor who began to chip off the extra rock from the original Image.

The child had found what was being longed all these years. Instantly, all the poisons were thrown away, all ill feelings got washed away, all hurts got healed, all pains gave relief, all misunderstandings got vanished, all brokenness disappeared with the act of apology and forgiveness and ultimately got to know one another and became one.

Several minutes passed, hours too, while the father continuously poured out his heart and explained where, how and why he went wrong. The child understood somewhat, if not everything, and the most important one is the realization and the next step for better living of both.

The inspector wanted to take his child back home but the rehabilitation therapists and the counselors requested him to let them continue with some more sessions and required care and counseling from their side. Agreeing to their terms he headed home. Everyone around was surprised and also got amazed to see the wonder working power of love, affection, realization and forgiveness. and also, the right way of their expression.

Having such great attributes is not just enough, having them in huge amounts and quantities is also not enough but having them utilized in the proper manner even in little amounts is most important, since that can only pass through all the hurt, troubled, suffered areas of life and perform their healing, mending, shaping, transforming, binding and reuniting tasks.

The worlds have failed to produce, accommodate and arrest such divine attributes in them, since the people with coolants and diffusers are very few on this thickly populated earth. The inspector who came to his original and needful senses firstly released all the hot pressure filled in him beyond measures, diffused all the explosives he planted in himself and then he took the initiative to release the hot air from his child and also diffuse the misunderstanding power. Anything done voluntarily, willfully and happily has tremendous working capacity to shake the foundations of unwilling, stubborn, and impossibilities.

The mother of just missed genius kept her promise and presented her child before the inspector accordingly the very next day, who turned out to be fortunate and received the compassion and soft corner from him. Since, the mother of just missed genius was the turning point for the inspector to realize and repent, he saw that a word of concern would work rather than action according to the law or a warning before release, and so sent the child away along with the mother and others present.

Now the inspector volunteered himself not only to see his child back in normal health but also to see the just missed genius too back in track. Therefore, he began to cater to both and see what best he can do to rehabilitate, motivate, educate, empower, and prepare them to volunteer to face the challenge that dragged them both against the nature, direction and system of living. But before that he follows the manual Mastering Myself to raise the banner of triumph himself.

Ending with the case studies that lead to many areas of improvement, control, education, enlightenment, and empowerment, we close this topic with a question, 'if you were the inspector and both the geniuses, just missed and totally missed are your children, how would you be dealing and what you would be doing to help their senses work properly, systematically and perfectly?' Keep thinking as we will have a glance through the final lessons from Mastering Myself Manual.

Lesson 19
Hell Bent Powers – Wise Supremacy

Moving straight away through the climax pages of Mastering Myself Manual, we are heading towards few more endless lists. Since, these lists specify particularly each thing needing to be mastered, the author felt to touch the psychological need of the reader by listing endless I ams and don'ts.

I'm angry, because you made me so. I'm angry because I got failed. I'm angry because my parents always compare me with you. I'm angry because you are supposed to wake me up, see I got late and missed my work. Do you have any idea how much I lost?

I'm angry because my mom didn't cook my taste foods. I'm angry because my wife doesn't respect me. I'm angry because my husband doesn't love me. I'm angry because my dad scolded me. I'm angry because you didn't allow me wear my choice dress. I'm angry because you didn't gift me anything on my birthday.

I'm angry because you didn't put me in the best school. I'm angry because I don't have a bike to go to college. I'm angry because you make me do things that I don't like. I'm angry because you force me for family and social gatherings, which I hate. I'm angry because you always scold me, even when I don't do anything wrong.

I'm angry because you thoughtlessly punish me for others' mistakes and wrongs. I'm angry because your love for my siblings is greater than mine. I'm angry because my friends teased me. I'm angry because I was bullied. I'm angry because my teacher has several pets in the class. I'm angry because you don't allow me to visit grandparents.

I'm angry because you misbehave with others. I'm angry because you don't allow me to chat with my friends. I'm angry because you still enforce your conservative thoughts on me. I'm angry because I didn't complete my homework. I'm angry because you took away my freedom.

I'm angry because you think I am still a kid. I'm angry because you don't trust me. I'm angry because I don't look good. I'm angry because your discipline suffocates me. I'm angry because I have several reasons. I'm angry because I don't need any reason for that.

Listing some 'I ams,' here and connecting the same with the list of bewares, dynamites and ultimatums, following usual but wrong practices is next step before standing in front of the mirror for right doings.

I'm angry so don't cross my way. I'm angry so don't trouble me. I'm am irritated, so don't make me mad anymore. I'm angry so be in your limits. I'm angry so mind your business. I'm angry so don't blame me for the consequences you will see for adding fuel to the fire.

I don't know what I will do when I am mad. So, beware. I don't even listen to myself once my head is heated up. I care no one, not even consider your age, so better stay away from me. I get blind in my madness, so anything in my hand at that moment will not know any bounds. So, it is up to you whether to continue maddening me or quit here.

My frustration levels are at peak, please leave me, else I am not responsible for the outburst. If you provoke me, you will see my taste. Don't dare do that. If you are stubborn, I am mad, crack, nut. I have a mood swing, sometimes exceeds the limits of human, even you might see the beast and the demon in me. So, I warn you beforehand. Why should you cross my way when you know I will no more be a human in my fiery state?

Sometimes, parents, spouses, siblings, relatives, friends, others in the vicinity become others' spokespersons and warn about their tempers and temperaments. Be careful s/he is not in a good mood, mad at the moment, disturbed, troubled, at loss, pain, suffered and the reactions will be dangerous, expensive and mad.

S/he is so friendly, loving, caring, respectful and obedient when in good mood, but you will see witches dancing on their heads in bad moods. So, better stay away from them and protect your honor, respect and dignity. I am not responsible if they misbehave with you. Look, I have warned you in advance.

These kinds of prides usually when supported by others rather than correcting, teaching, rebuking and disciplining them automatically turns out to be their own snares at some point of time, and could possibly be forever a thorn in their fleshes. It could be because they don't know how to put them in control, they don't feel it is necessary, they don't mind such behavior, they have no issues with it as along as it doesn't affect them, they are least bothered about the outcomes of others reactions for the same or they really take pride to be on the side of such strong powered fierce people.

Coming to the last part of Mastering Myself, here's what one has to do to really master all such powers, forces, energies, thoughts, actions, reactions, and wild behaviors by following the right way of dealing. This is the last coolant, final diffuser, ultimate absorber and climaxing pressure releaser, so, let's have a look at it and say good bye to our masters (reactors/explosives) who ruled over us all these years and decades.

Do you still want to consider them your masters of your choice, they are good and your benefactors, then you can go ahead continuing the same, else dethrone them right now and you take the Master's seat and be enthroned to rule over all your powers? Decide to have the controlling authority by an easy method of self-introspection and self-proclamation.

I am angry but won't allow it to be stored in me which can cause outburst. In my anger I won't allow anyone to add fuel and provoke me further. I will no longer disrespect others, let them be even younger to me, because everyone has his/her self-respect to be protected. I have no right to hurt anyone.

Why should others suffer due to my bad temper? Why should others bear my tantrums? Why should I lose my cool? Why should I heat myself up to the levels of madness? Why should I be the reason for someone's peace, happiness, laughter, joy, good moods disappear from their hearts and faces? Who gave me the right to snatch away others best assets?

I know I am frustrated, but I will go to the roots of its reasons and follow systematic way to remove it from my heart. I will ask the depression to vacate my house by showing the powerful, positive, healthy side of living, which actually was affected by the wrong, painful, helpless and hopeless side of life. I will no longer give way to disappointment make steps into my enthusiastic, energetic and zealous heart. I will teach my senses to resist the temptations that will ruin my life with shame and guilt.

I knew now how to say no to anything that lures me with illicit, unlawful, immoral and seductive powers. Since I have no right to enter into others' lives with destructive schemes, I say that none of such have the right to convince, market and sell their schemes to destroy me.

I knew today, all that glitters is not gold, all that proclaims my friends and well-wishers are truly not the same but they find ways to befriend me and occupy my mind, heart, senses and thoughts and leave me to suffer for their actions physically, mentally, emotionally, financially and in many other ways.

I know I am being ruled by bad powers, but I won't let my anger, irritation, frustration, disappointment, short temper, tantrums, harsh, bad, wrong behaviors, attitudes, moods and mood swings affect, reflect or play on others. Let that be anyone, by doing so I am at the path of making baby but perfect steps towards Mastering Myself.

And I am sure that it is my confidence, my stable, constant and continuous walk in the same path that gave gutsy vocals to declare that I am the Master over Myself and wish all the readers too, a successful and victorious Mastering Myself, your secret to subdue hell bent powers.

9 789393 388971

Printed by Libri Plureos GmbH in Hamburg, Germany